FROM THE EYES OF EGYPT

An Artistic Reflection

Lisa Camacho

Art by Karim Emad

ISBN 979-8-89345-572-4 (paperback)
ISBN 979-8-89345-574-8 (digital)

Christian Faith Publishing
832 Park Avenue
Meadville, PA 16335
www.christianfaithpublishing.com

Printed in the United States of America

What is written on the brow will inevitably
be seen by the eye.

—Egyptian proverb

To Artist Karim Emad as your love, dedication, knowledge, and artistic craft has given me the gift to envision the motherland of Egypt from afar. Your spirit and creative essence have given me the courage to pursue my art of writing, to hear my heart, and find my voice. I am grateful for your sacrifice and patience while completing this book for the glory of God because He gave you life and a talent that will continue to touch the lives of others around the world!

INTRODUCTION

As a child, I was fascinated with the images of Egypt and how its history invaded all the world's existence. In church, I learned about it by studying the book of Exodus in the Bible. In school, I learned about the Nile River and the powerful influences of Cleopatra. The beauty of the pyramids, its culture, and its people finally touched me in high school, when I met my first Egyptian friend, a charming and beautiful girl named Angela that my heart could never forget. She returned to Egypt with her family in the summer of 1994. I still remember how I cried goodbye, and that the only word that brought me comfort was when she looked at me and said, "Do not worry, my dear friend Lisa. I will never forget you, and one day, you can come to Egypt."

Several years later, while studying in the university, I met remarkable Egyptian professors that grasped my attention with their wisdom and intelligence. These experiences simply increased my interest and love for Egypt. In 2017, I had attended a conference at Asbury Seminary regarding Islam and how to establish open dialogue with those of the Muslim faith. It was an insightful event that sparked other interests regarding the Middle Eastern traditions, cultures, languages, and spiritual beliefs. Each personal encounter and experience were meaningful and significant in its own right.

In 2020, the COVID-19 pandemic gave me the blessing of virtual interaction through social media platforms that opened friendship opportunities from around the world, including that of the motherland of Egypt. All friends are unique, especially when meeting them though social media platforms. My new Egyptian friends had deepened my curiosity and intrigue to know Egypt. However, others with great intentions had only given me a romanticized view of Egypt. Yet, within me, I was looking for the reality of modern Egypt and all its beauty. It was a secret prayer in my heart to meet a person that would listen to my thoughts, address my questions, and cause me to truly fall in love with Egypt. It was important since I have never seen Egypt with my own eyes. My soul longed to know and touch Egypt, despite the distance.

In December 2022, my prayer for Egypt and my endless desire to know it was answered through my first meeting with artist Karim Emad. In our first conversation, I knew that my search was over because Karim was so authentic and real through his artwork. I knew that I had met a gifted man but also that I found the eyes of Egypt, eyes that you can investigate and read the soul and trust. As months passed us, the artwork of Karim Emad simply captivated my heart and imagination because through it I could see Egypt like never before. In his artwork, I have discovered the voices of modern Egyptians, a generation of people that live with ultimate hope, faith, and love. The art of Karim Emad guides its beholder to understand the rawness and genuine spirit of Egypt.

As a Christian woman that has never visited Egypt, I realized that God had opened the windows of heaven, when I reflected on Karim's art as all his paintings have taught me to further pursue God, hope, love, beauty, and the need to seek righteousness and justice. The mystery and power of art is its ability to give us expression—an expression that is nonverbal but leads me to a deeper reflection that enhances my written expression.

This book is not an academic masterpiece but a reflective montage of how my reality of Egypt has been shaped through the artwork of Karim Emad. Under no terms do I claim to be an expert in art or its historical context, but through my personal growth and genuine relationship with Karim Emad, I have created understanding of the power of art and how it can reveal the strongest feelings within the soul. Art can speak about feelings, people, places, religions, and cultures. It can become the voice that breaks the silence. My conversations with Karim unfolded my heart and unlocked the depth of my feelings to love Egypt and place in it my soul without setting foot into this beautiful country.

Karim has taught me not to be afraid to speak of God, my life experiences, and the dreams that lie within me, to believe in love and myself. His constant encouragement and ongoing collaboration have provoked me to develop my own gift through the art of writing. He focused on our similarities, and love is greater than any differences that could exist between us. The differences that others may observe between us such as culture, religion, traditions, and age have become obsolete between us as we have shared life experiences about family, tradition, culture, religion, and art. One might say that God brought us together through the gift of art, and our bonding has been perfected in our hearts.

Because of my endless gratitude, I decided to create this book that recognizes the gift that God has placed in Karim Emad's life through his artwork and existence. I also believe that his artwork will continue to expand and touch the hearts of so many around the world. So let us begin the fascinating artistic journey that I discovered through the eyes of Egypt.

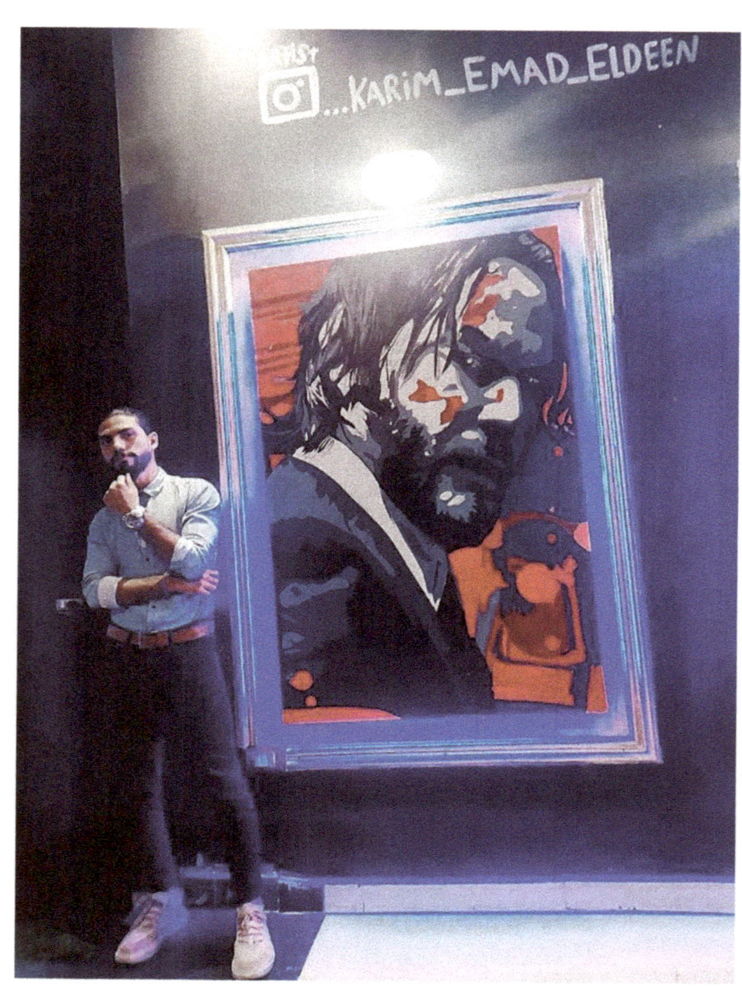

The artist, Karim Emad

CHAPTER 1

Egypt is not a country we live in but
a country that lives within us.

—Pope Shenouda III

Karim Emad was born and raised in Cairo, Egypt, and at twenty-five years old, his talent continues to reach great heights. His talent in the arts has touched various venues in Egypt. His paintings are presented beyond the scopes of canvas and sketchbooks. Karim has delighted the streets of Egypt and other locations with his artwork. Karim's artistic voice is one of authenticity, ambition, social reality, and beauty. In conversation, I asked Karim, "Why did you become an artist?"

He responded, "It was God's destiny for me. I did not choose it, but it chose me."

The artwork represents Karim Emad's personality that is resilient, versatile, intellectual, and filled with emotional intelligence.

In my enthusiasm for admiring his artwork, I also became interested in his personal beliefs and traditions as he was raised Muslim and in a large family. I observed his loving and industrious nature while living daily struggles. His humility and willingness to engage in candid conversations caused me to want to know more about his art and life perspectives. To unfold the resiliency of his spirit and passion for art and life became a priority. He seemed to possess the answers that I always wrestled with regarding love, time, social structures, religions, and politics. In many ways, he revealed it all through explaining his artwork and life experiences. I felt a heartfelt connection because I realized that at the core of our hearts existed gratitude for God, and our love for art had united us. Karim had become my person, my eagle, and my greatest teacher about the Egyptian world. And I questioned myself: Did destiny also bring us together?

My person

The truth is that what drives a person's passion is also the channel of deep influence to reach the lives of others. For Karim, art is everything, and he acknowledges it to be his timeless passion. Through the sharing of his art, he also unlocked my heart because I found his passion intriguing and purposeful. I would inquire about a particular painting or drawing, and he would indulge me with the methods and motivations behind its creation. In fact, our first conversation developed because Karim asked, "Lisa, do you like art?"

He explained that individuals that enjoy art tend to be reflective, creative, and highly intelligent. He also explained that all people possess an artistic ability, but we need to search for it and develop our skills. Even though I do not have an artistic ability for painting or drawing, I did begin to question myself: Do I have a great passion? What is everything to me in life? When these questions provoked me to examine the deepest longings of my heart and my purpose, I came to the realize that Karim is "my person." Despite his introspective personality, Karim Emad is willing to share his wisdom, knowledge, feelings, and talents. He was the person that I could connect with, whether my day was victorious or horrendous. He would give me the space to voice my concerns, questions, and feelings. Frequently, he would teach me about the importance of critical thinking but also to exercise boundaries. He recommended that I should learn how to become a "closed box." I understood that Karim is a closed box that possesses diverse gifts beyond the talent of art. We discovered that despite our different worlds, Karim and I are similar in congruent ways. Below is the first picture that Karim Emad shared from his art collection with me.

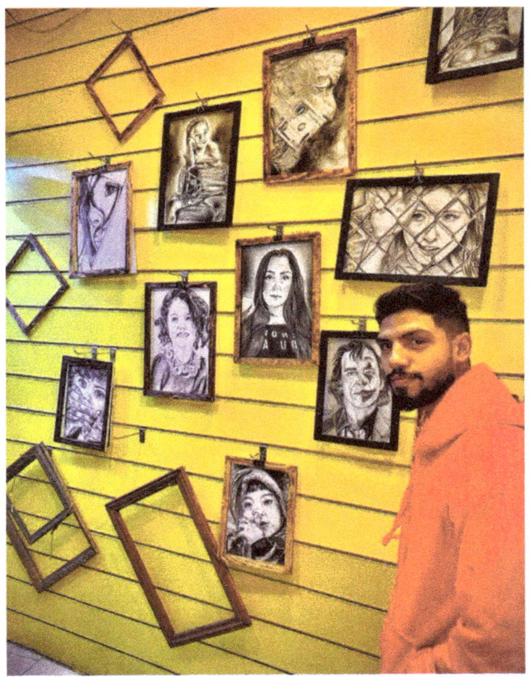

My teacher

In embracing the magical world of Egypt, I hoped that I would find a teacher that would guide me in the ways of the land. There is a Japanese proverb that says that "better than a thousand days of diligent study is one day with a great teacher." I had studied the life, culture, and religious belief systems in Egypt but always felt that something was missing. The gap was Karim Emad, the personal encounter that made all my knowledge come alive. He taught me discernment in the midst of Egyptian culture. Karim also eliminated numerous myths that I had adopted as truths regarding the Islamic lifestyle. The teacher influenced by mental images what life truly is in the wonderful land of Egypt. He also said that even if I could not understand the Arabic language, it was fine because I could surely feel it in my heart.

Karim Emad did exactly that in this virtual learning experience. He provided interpretation where I could find no words to explain my love for Egypt and its enchanting people. He encouraged me to observe people, places, and images with a loving heart but not to disregard the existence of criticism. How I viewed Egypt was with a historical perspective but also with a narrow eye. The artwork and sharing of common life with Karim made me uncover the layers of a modern and traditional culture all in one. The work ethic, the family bonds, the unfailing faith, and its mesmerizing antique structures are just a few of the pillars in Egyptian life, regardless of social status, political, and religious differences. Egyptians preserve the beauty of life and seek to maintain authenticity in the face of modern culture. In conversations, Karim would always teach me that a person's eyes cannot lie because they are the real windows of a person's soul.

This artistic teacher also taught me about the beauty of true love. Karim Emad has exemplified that true love and a union between two people has no limits, much like what the Bible describes as unfailing love in 1 Corinthians 13, but this was beyond religious knowledge. I understood that God joined two hearts for different purposes and various perspectives. When love guides the interactions and conversations between two people, communication becomes an art. You learn to master the art of listening and carefully responding to each other. As a result, a person becomes more vulnerable and aware of his/her biases, leading to greater personal growth. In doing so, Karim has taught me that we can restore our faith and our love for humanity in general. For this reason, we cannot detain our opportunities to love and to be loved by another, just as a great artist never shies away from an empty canvas. Art is a symbol of hope for all people to find the power of expression in life.

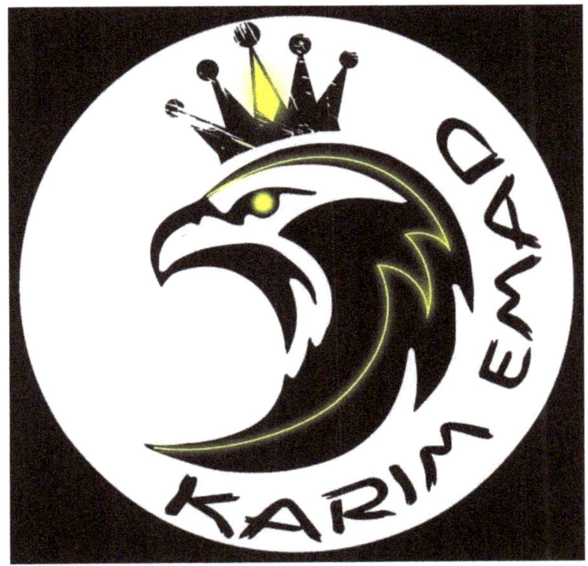

The Karim artwork logo

My eagle

The Bible teaches that the eagle is a symbol of power and signifies courage, strength, wisdom, and victory. The visualization of a soaring eagle has given me feelings of hope and inspiration. The symbol of an eagle has produced a confirmation of protection and freedom in the most difficult times of my life, the moments of life where everything has shattered at once, and you are only left with the broken pieces. When I felt that I could no longer rise, my thoughts reflected on the majestic eagle. The eagle rises to new heights in the midst of great adversity and storms. Like the eagle, I do believe that the storms of life can only lead to becoming stronger and finding more open doors of opportunity.

For this reason, when I met Karim Emad, I was not only struck by the versatility of his artwork, I was mesmerized with his brand that was represented by an eagle, the majestic bird that had captured my soul and heart from the time of my youth. The white feathers symbolize purity, and the golden eyes indicate transparency and vision. This moon-shaped eagle represents his Muslim faith, and the crown signifies his royal character. As I examined the beautiful eagle, I realized that God had placed Karim Emad in my life. The purpose was an unknown mystery to me, but I knew that God had orchestrated our divine appointment. In every chat, Karim spoke few words about his life, his art, his religion, and his Egypt. But the words were enough for me to interpret the messages and revelation. He demonstrated all the characteristics of an eagle as I often became the storm, a storm filled with questions, curiosity, and intrigue.

He possesses the patience and resilience to assist my imagination and understand human suffering with greater capabilities, so much that my heart begins to soften and yearned to know Egypt through his eyes, an Egypt that possesses intelligence, love, endurance, and submission. He unfolded a nation that is developed every day by creative and industrious people. They embrace loss and pain with profound resignation and dignity. He explained that our lives must always be filled with gratitude for God's will, regardless of our circumstances. He encouraged me to understand life and the eagle in its different seasons.

Karim has mastered the experiences related to life and death and the impact of social influence all at once! And I must say that Karim loves heights! He continues to rise through the innovation of his art but also because of his generous heart! This was evident as he shared his masterpieces, month after month, and causing me to reflect on the beauty of Egypt but also my own as an author. He explained that every person has a flight to embark and that fear should not detain our dreams because nothing can stop an eagle from reaching its destination.

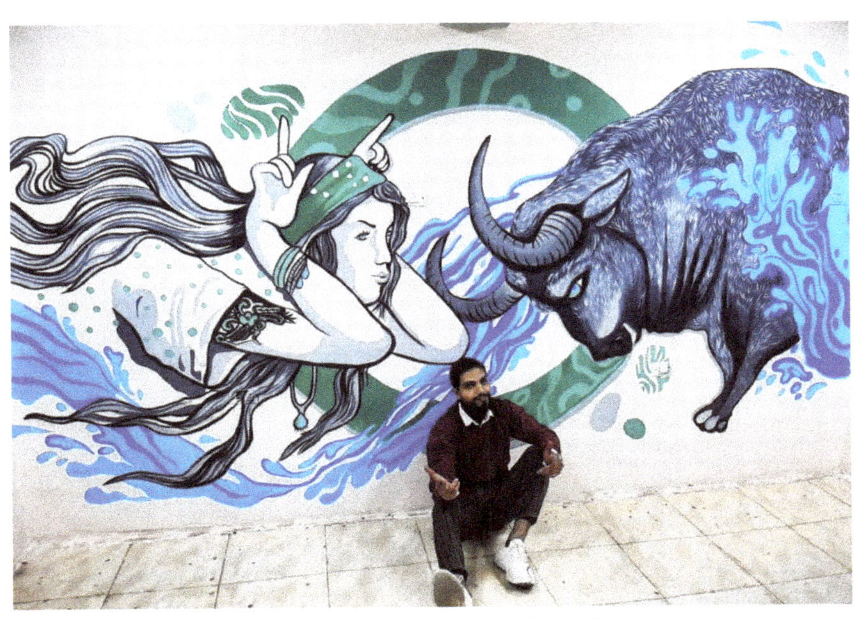

The People by Karim Emad

CHAPTER 2

Words are a pretext. It is the inner bond that
draws one person to another, not words.

—Rumi

As I studied Egyptian culture, I have discovered that Egyptian people are charming, humble, industrious, and dignified, and Karim Emad possesses all these characteristics. He also educated me on Egyptian etiquette and how to best communicate with men and women in his society. He explained that each person is different, and we must place close and careful attention to the world of others in general. But never forget to be yourself before all people because this world can be deceptive. There is an Egyptian proverb that depicts Karim's words, and it says, "Know the world in yourself. Never look for yourself in the world, for this would be to project your illusion."

The Egyptian people are tenacious and humorous in the face of hardships. They are loyal, romantic, and soulful when encountered with true and pure love. The people in the land of Egypt are full of dreams, mysteries, and memories. Karim Emad's artwork was my window to understanding the lives of the Egyptian people. Each illustration is an open gate to analyzing the life of every person he has painted in his career. Examining the paintings gave me the gift of personification, speculation, and interpretation. As I have exercised scrutiny with each painting, I received insight of the Egyptian people's personal pain, joy, and emotion. The experience made me reflect on how we define beauty and that the eyes truly are the windows to a person's soul. In this chapter, we will indulge in Karim Emad's artwork as he portrays the Egyptian people in modern ordinary life. His work reveals their ultimate beauty and genuine essence.

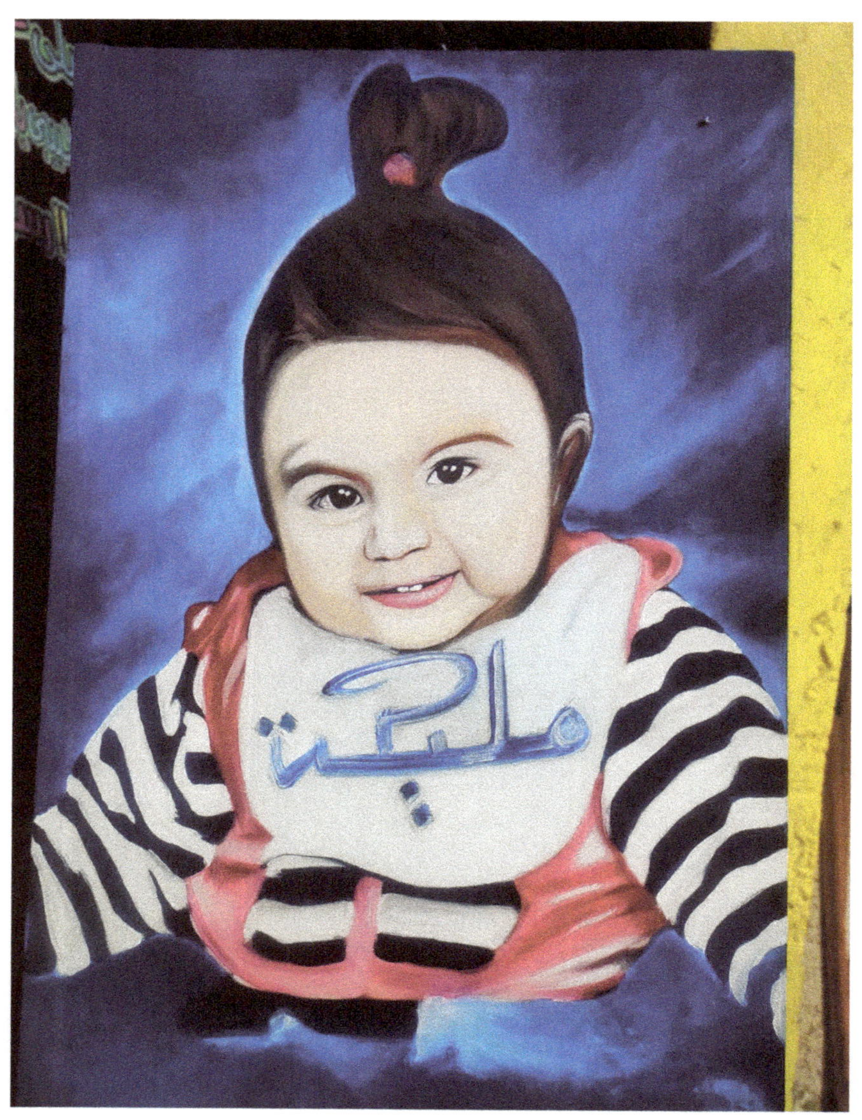

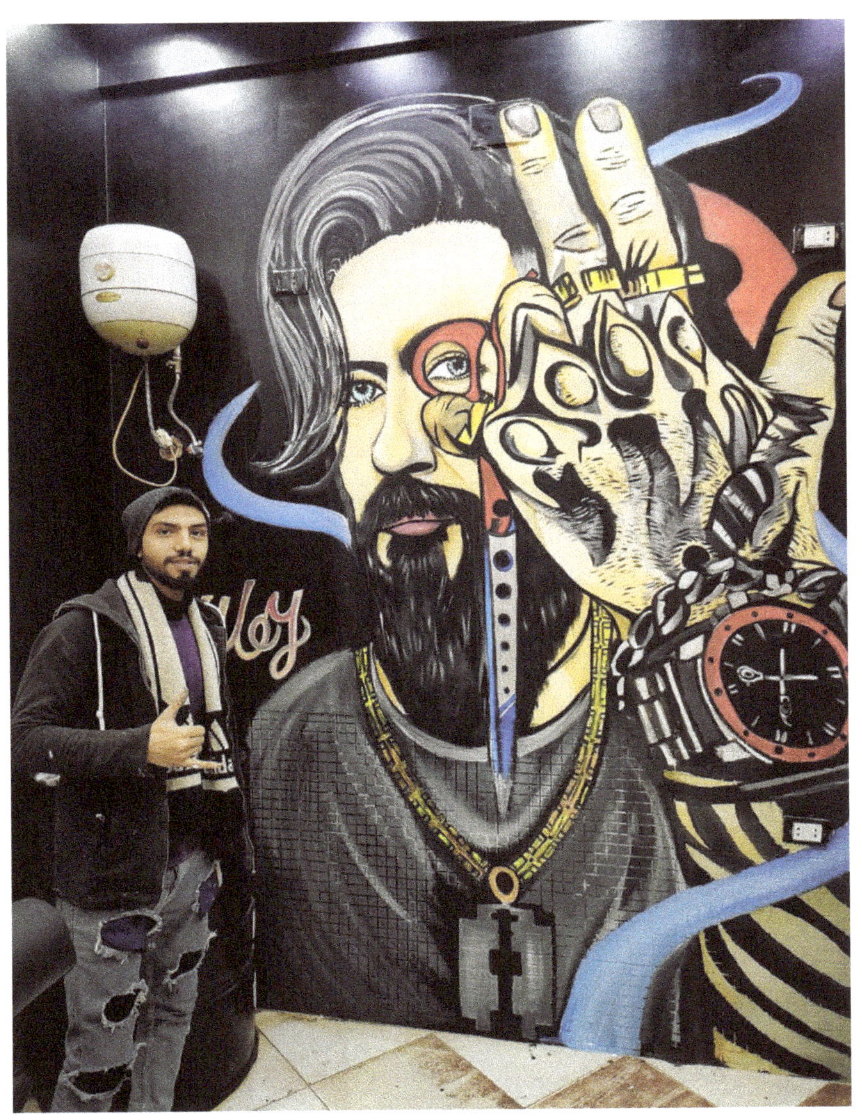

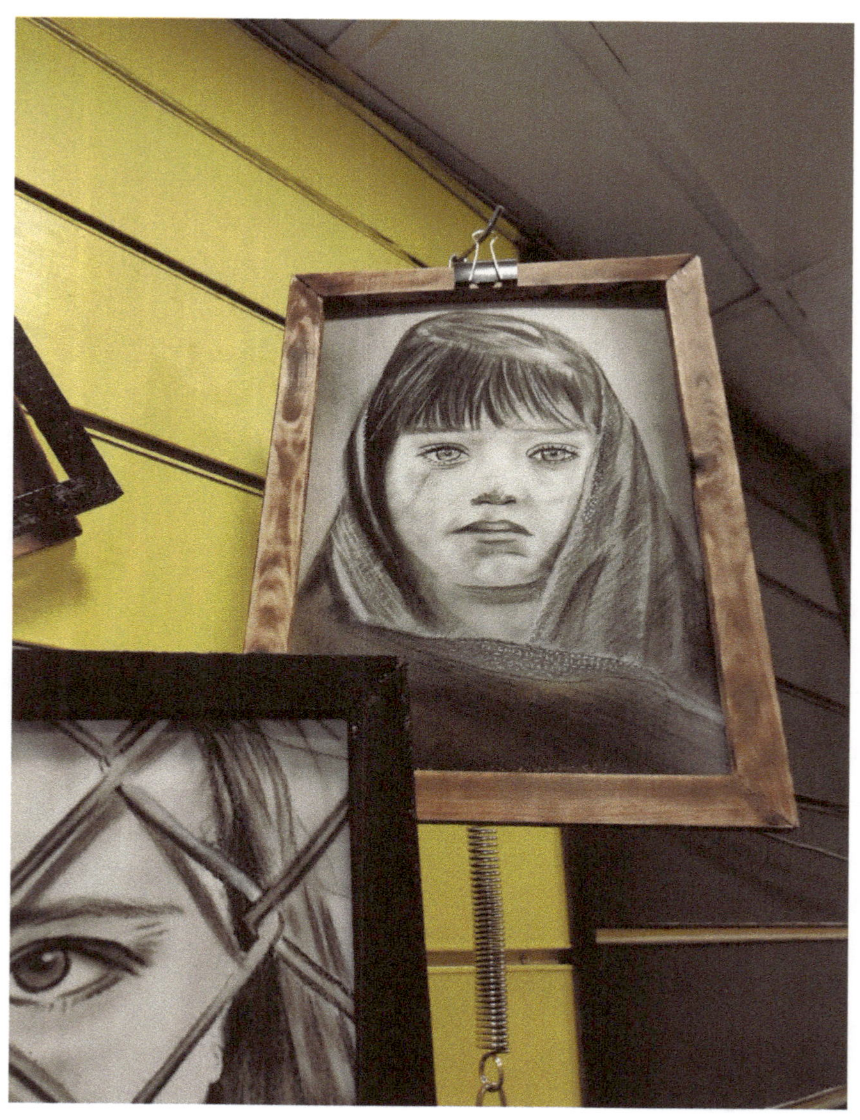

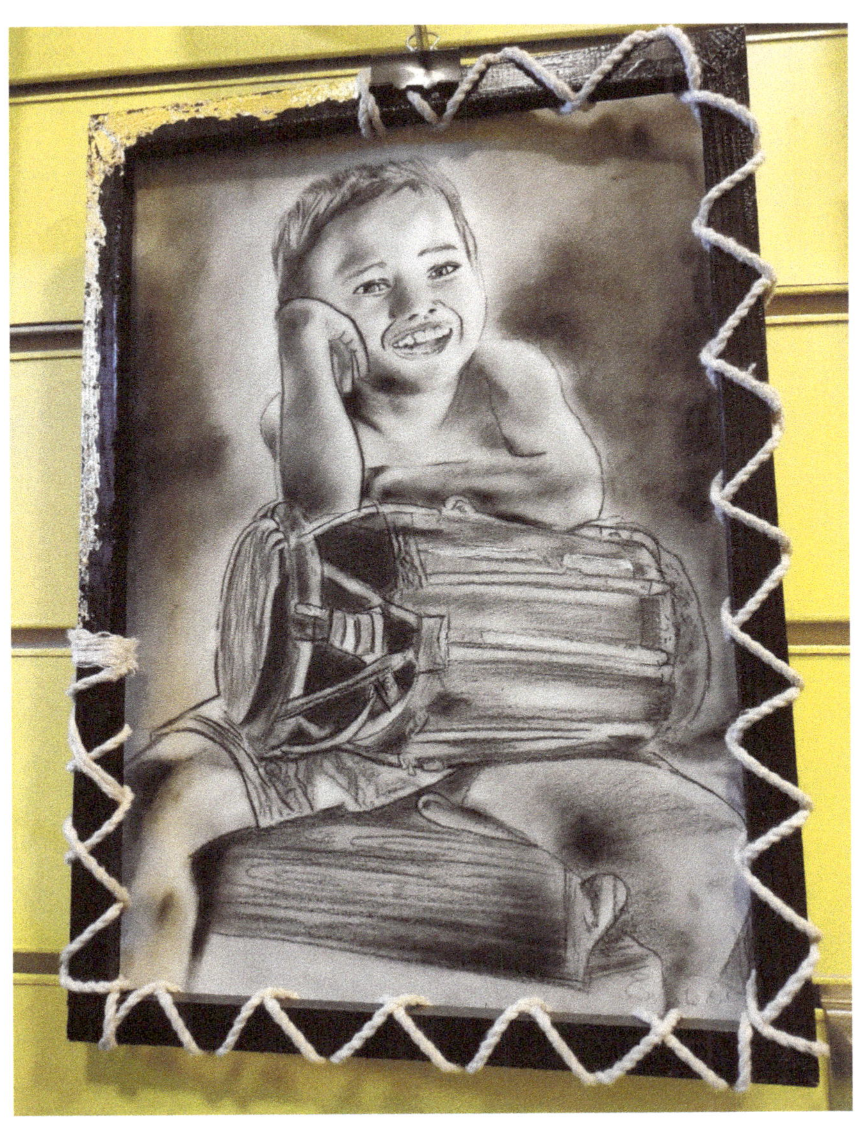

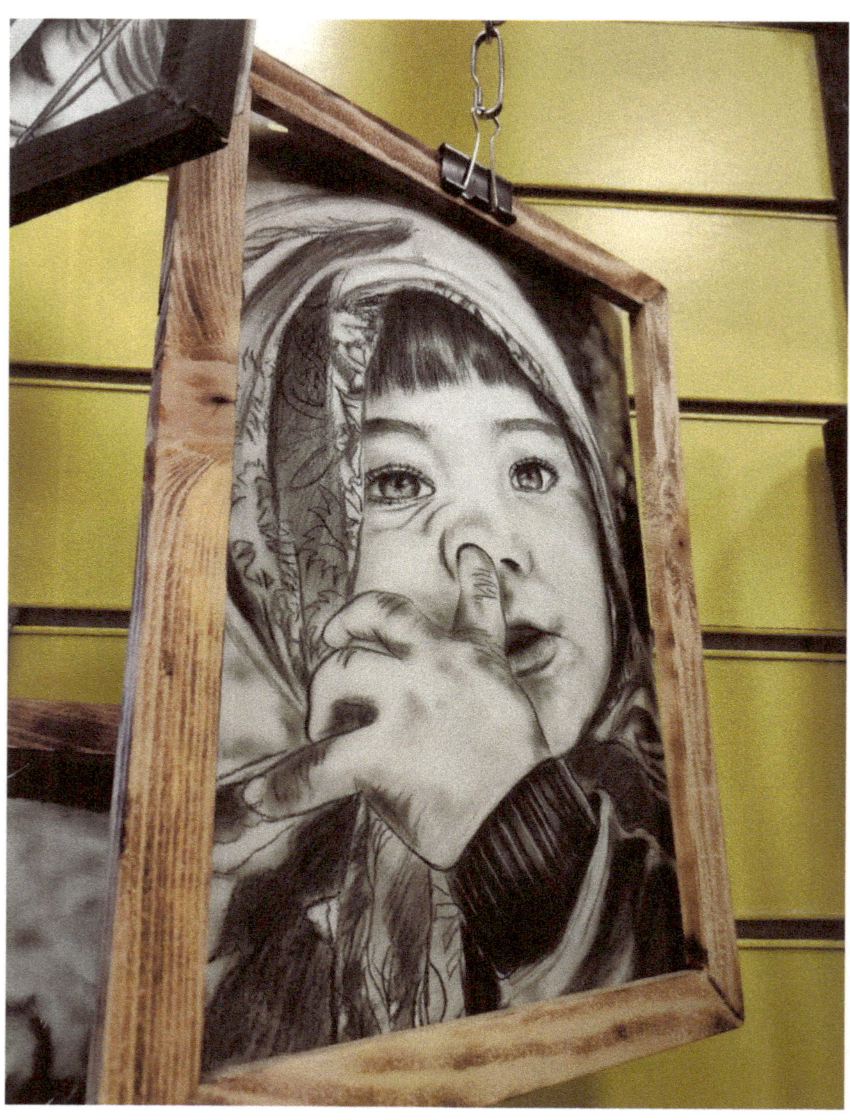

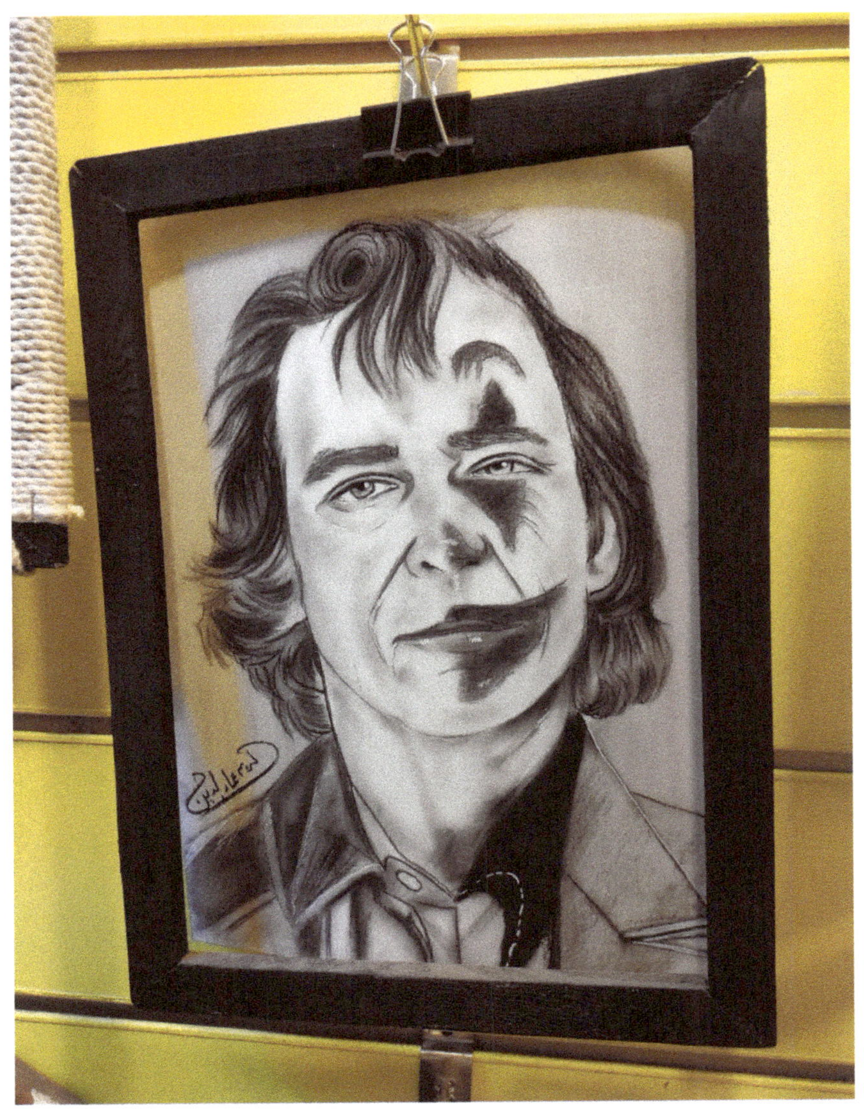

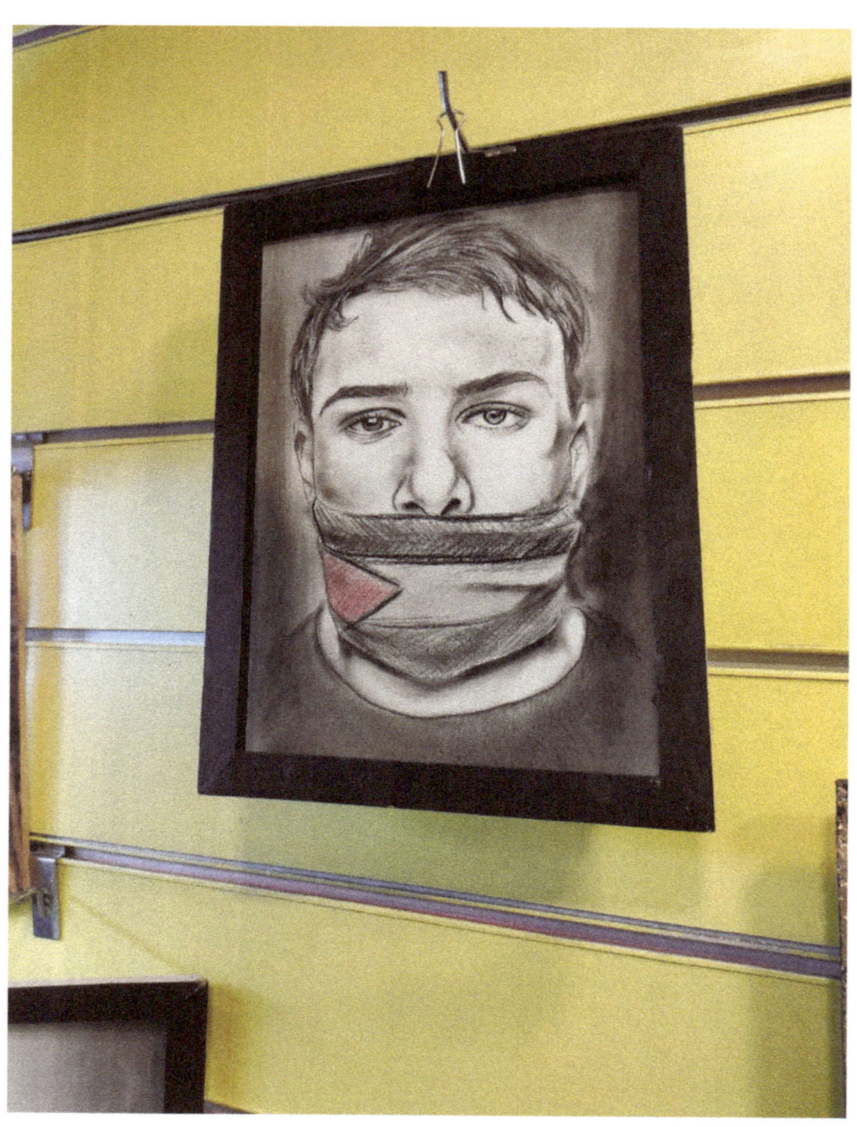

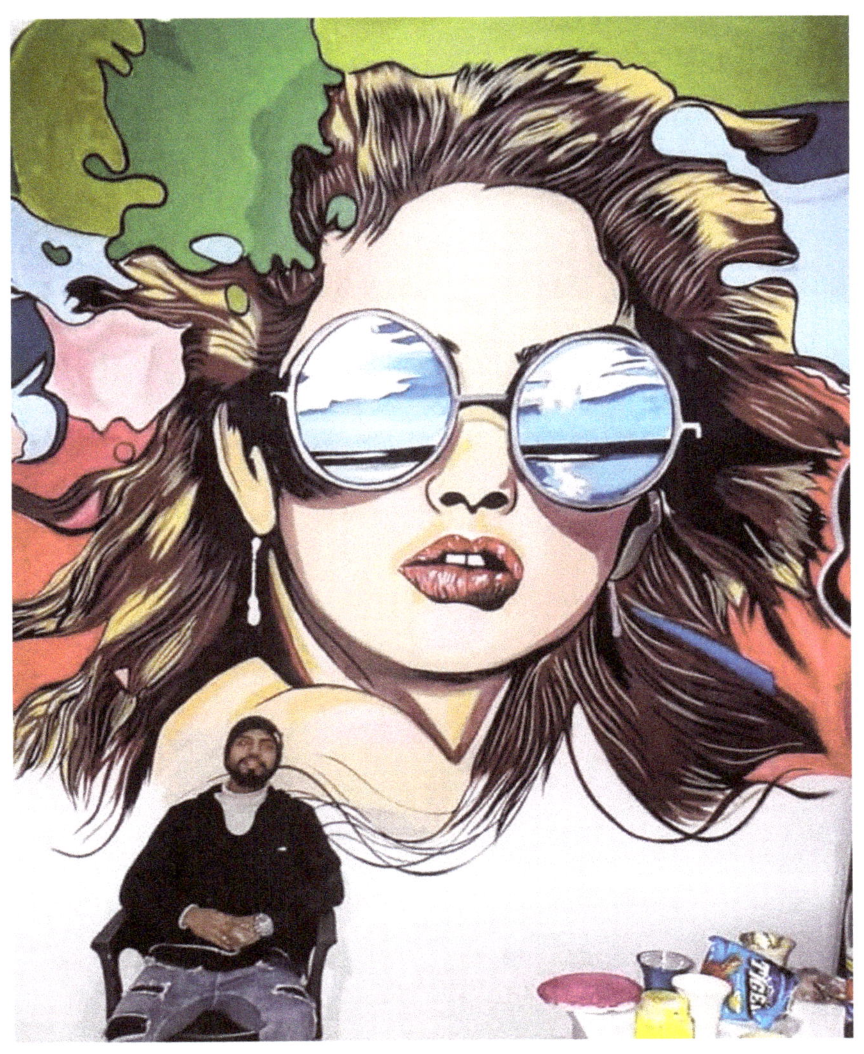

TWIGEE

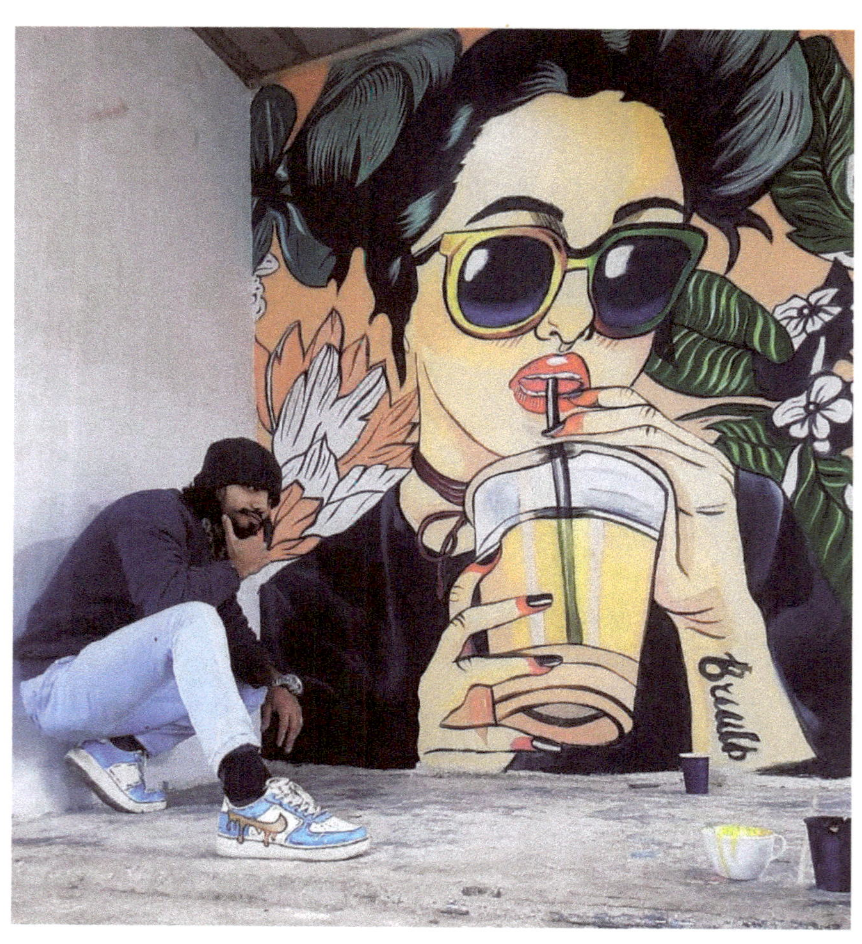

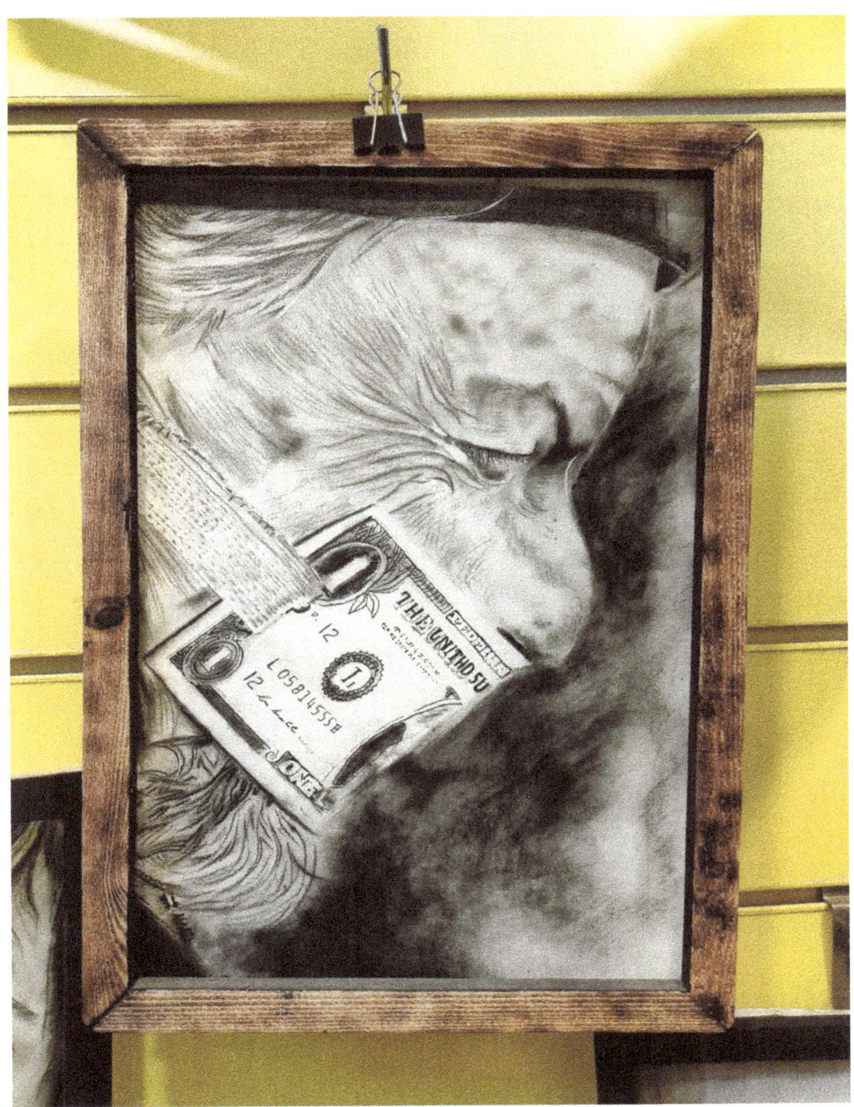
THE UNITED ST
L 05814555 B
ONE

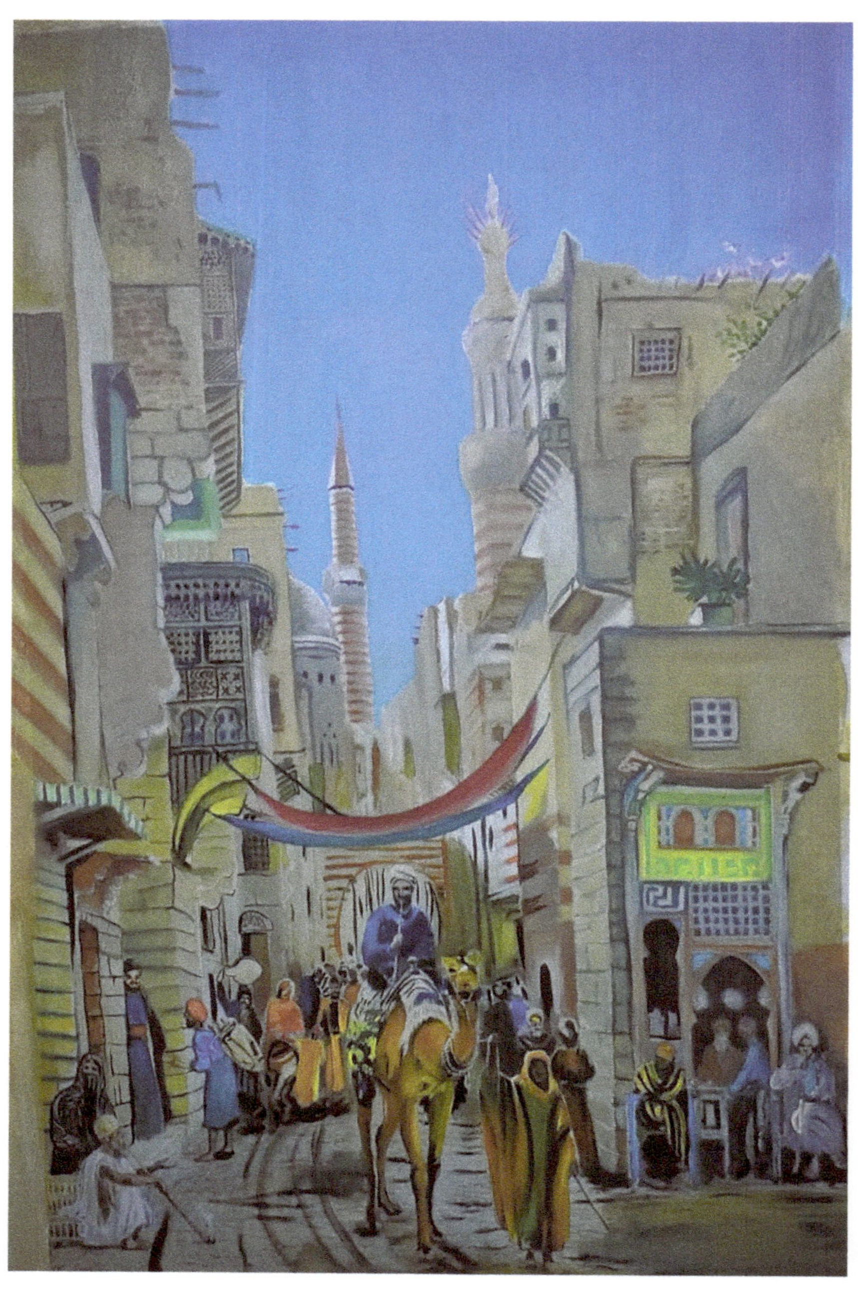

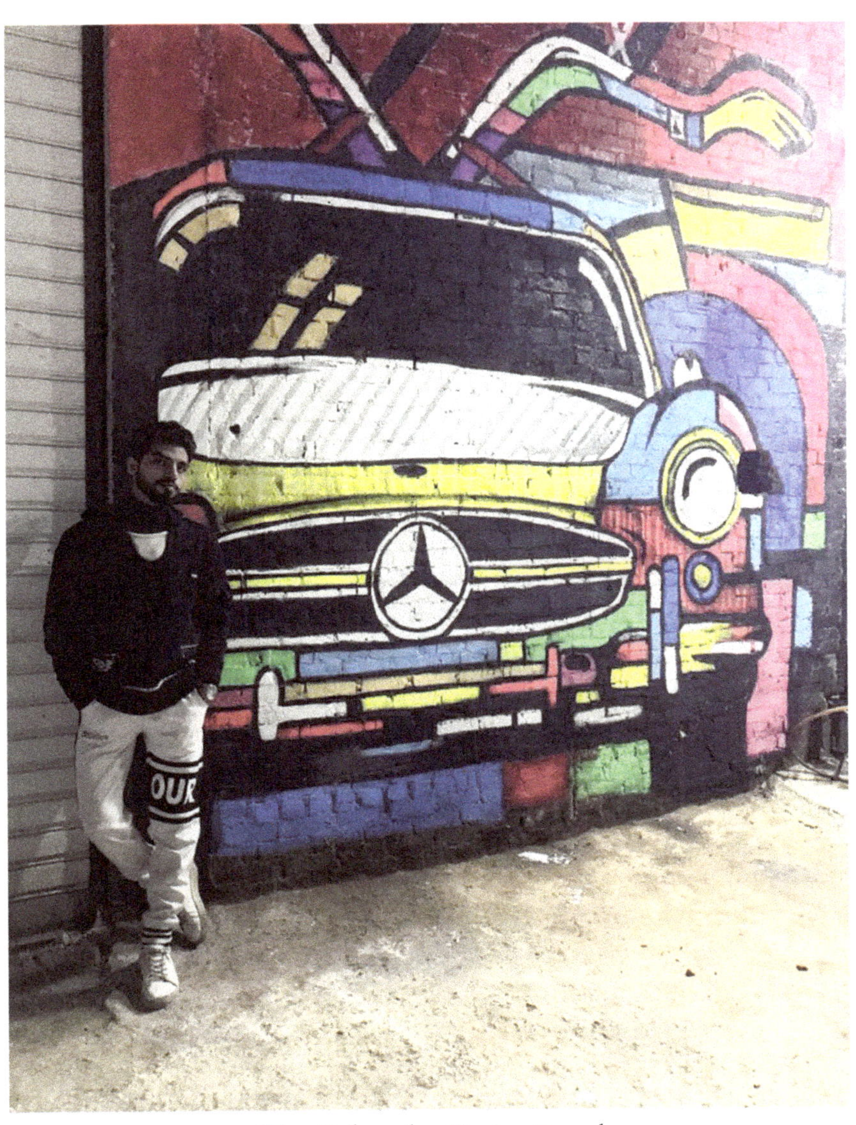

The Culture by Karim Emad

CHAPTER 3

Egypt is a treasure house of history, religion, and culture.

—Sharmeen Obaid-Chinoy

In my virtual connection with Karim Emad, I have seen this quote written by Sharmeen Obaid-Chinoy come to life. He taught me that Egyptian culture encompasses several factors: (1) pride; (2) honor; (3) loyalty; (4) modesty; (5) education; and (6) community. The Egyptian culture takes pride and status in being helpful, generous, and charitable with others. It is an unspoken expectation among all people to be loyal to their family. Men are also expected to treat others with utmost respect and keep their promises or verbal contracts at all times. Generally, Egypt can be described as a collectivist society. Therefore, the needs of the family or community surpass the personal needs of any particular individual. I observed this in my communication with Karim as he failed to express his personal desires regarding his artistic career, yet he continuously encouraged me to finish this book and felt honored that I had selected him as the artist for this project.

He expressed feelings of humility when I admired his latest masterpiece or art design. His artwork depicts the colors of Egypt and its vibrant culture. For Karim, the beauty of his motherland Egypt will remain a source of inspiration as we will see in the next pages in this chapter.

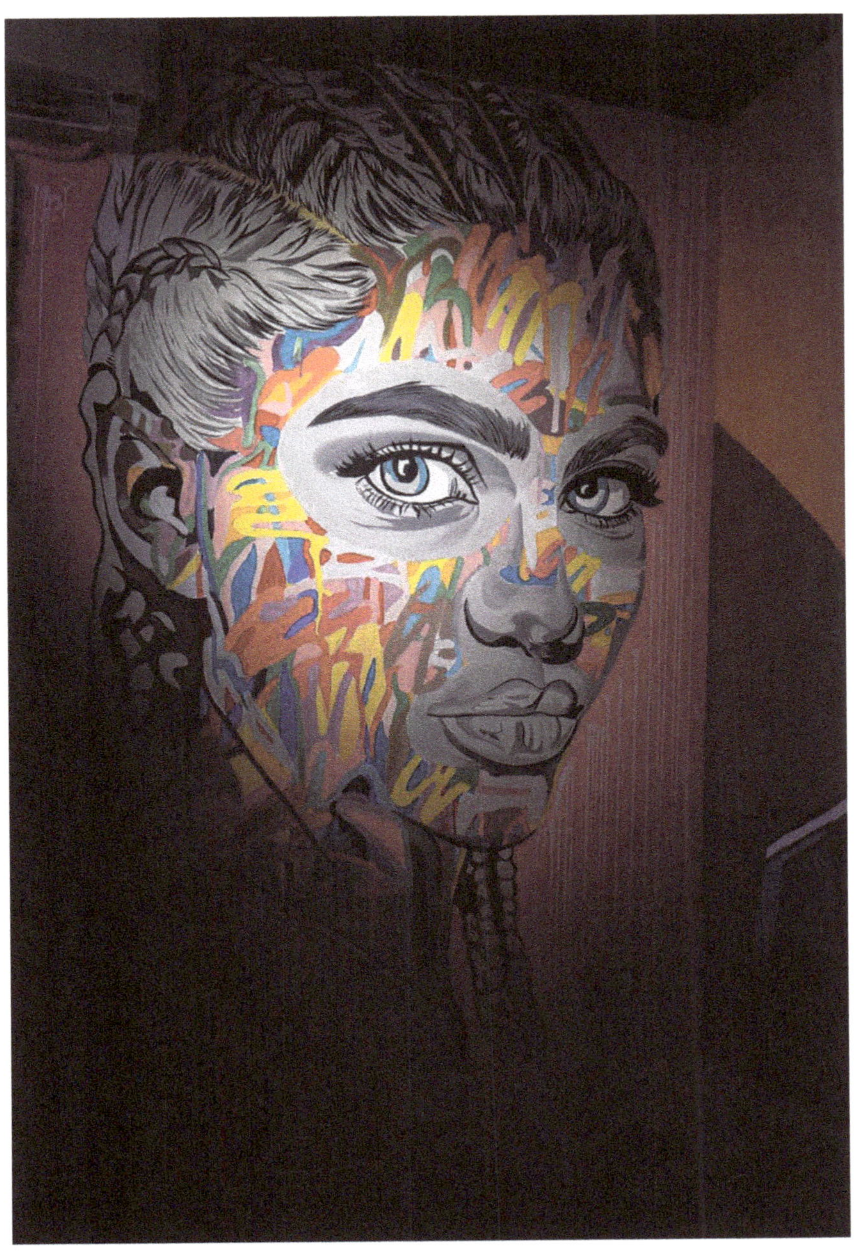

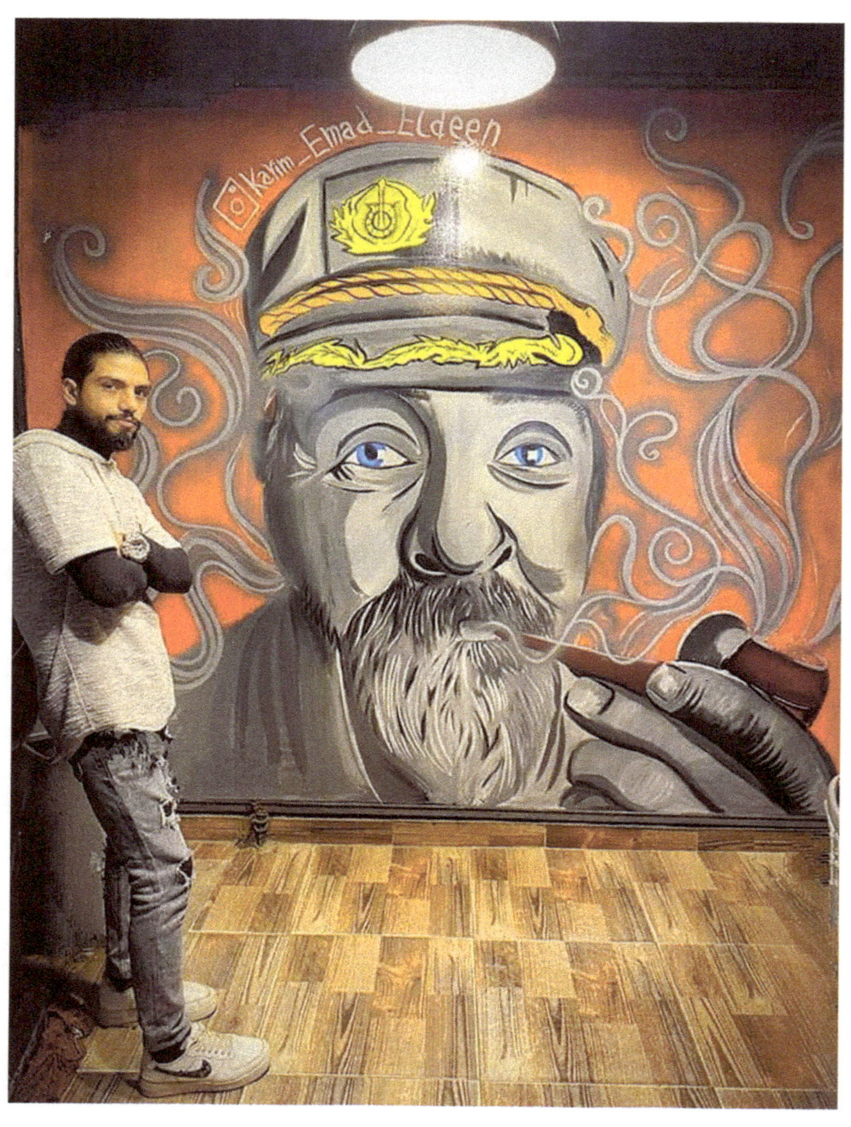

Karim_Emad_Eldeen

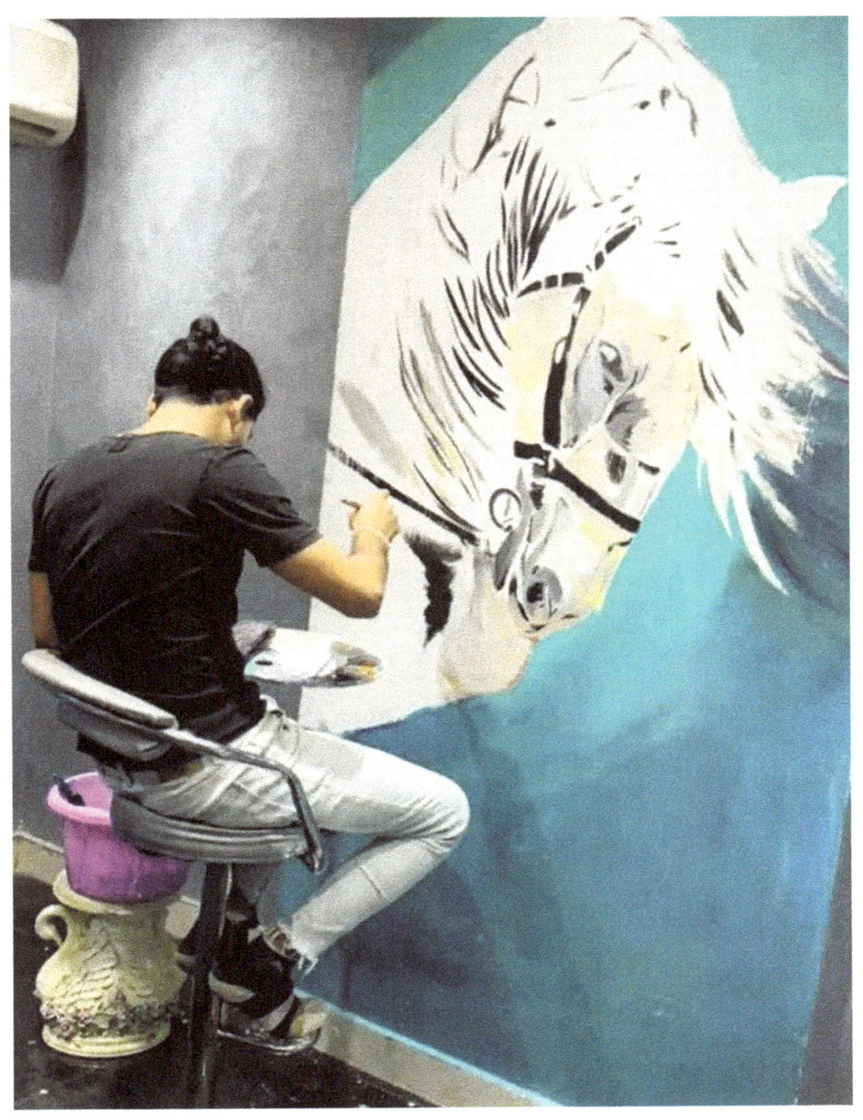

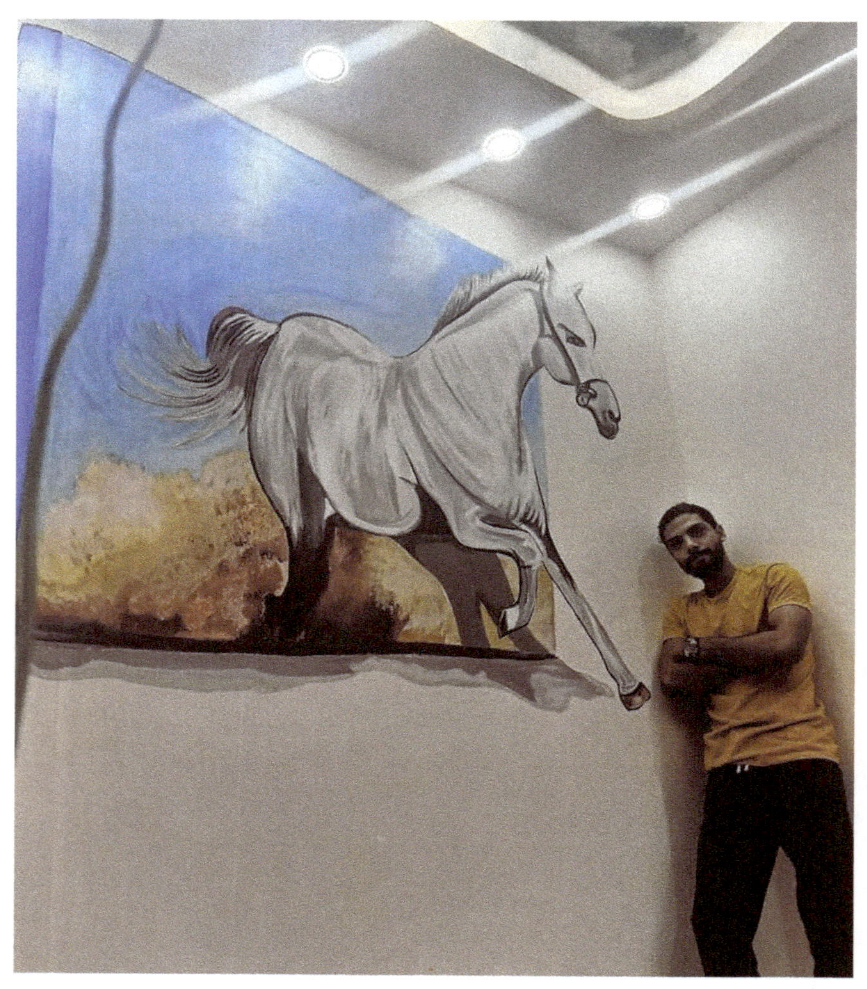

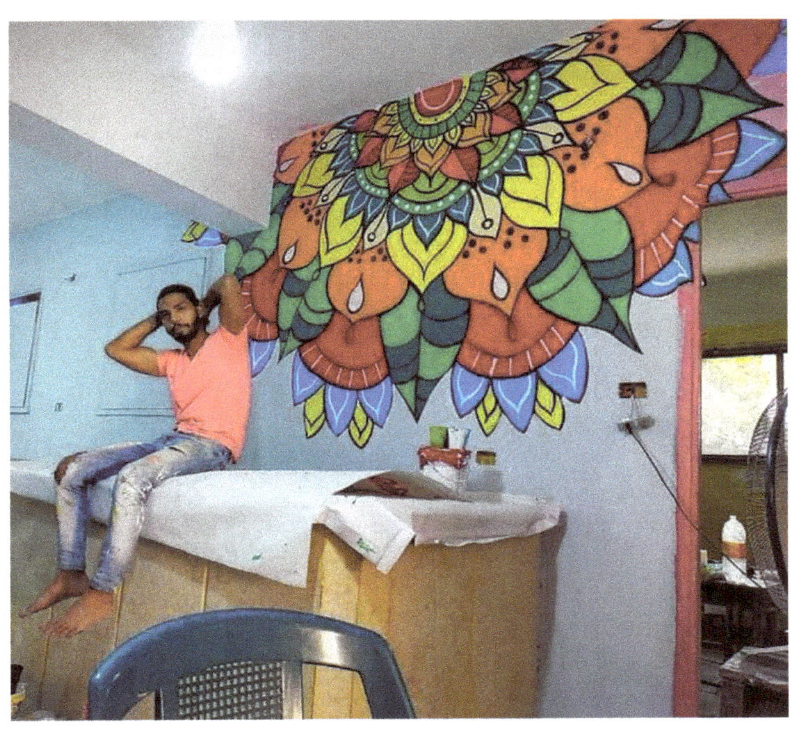

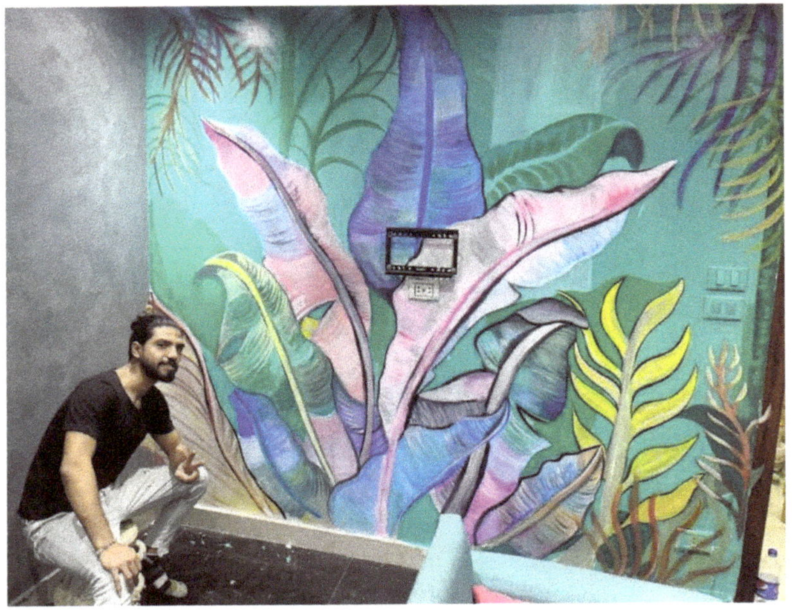

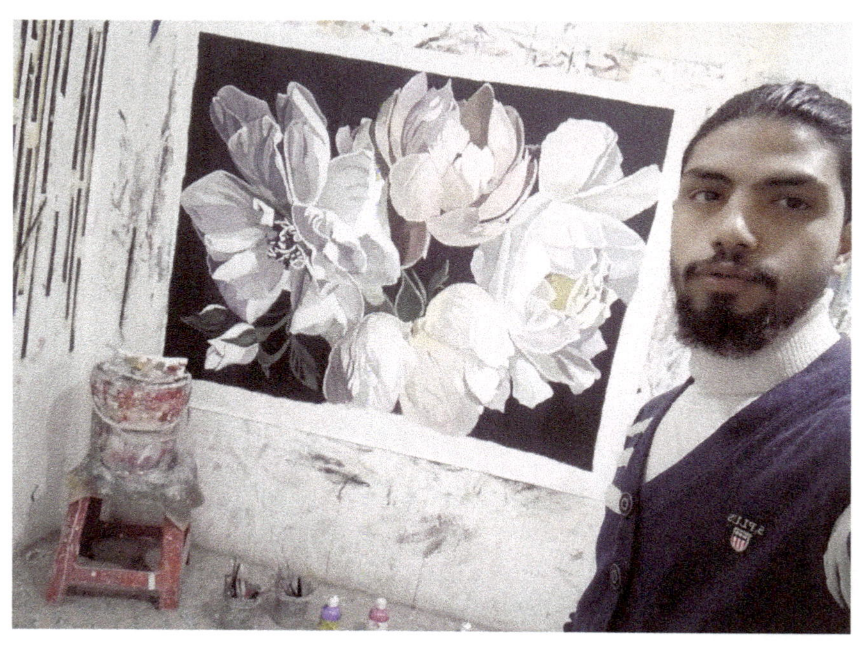

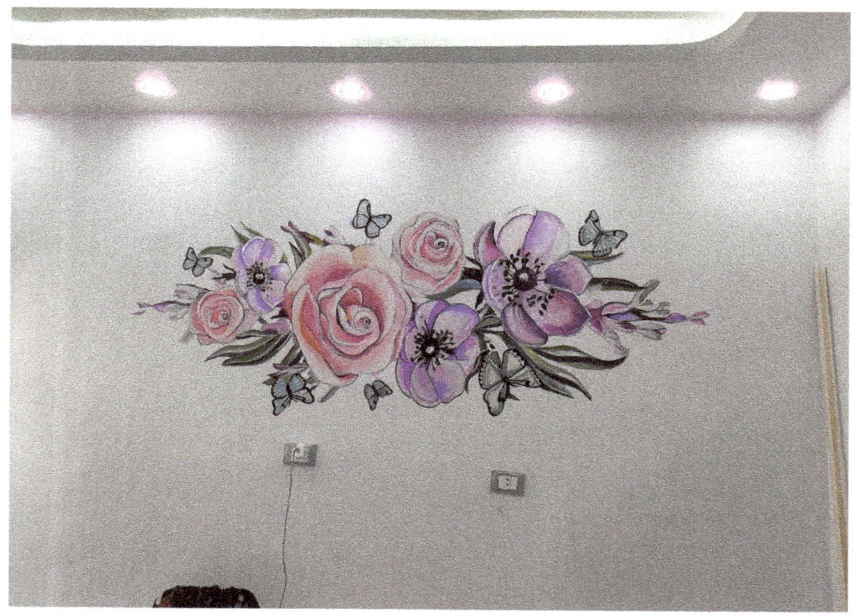

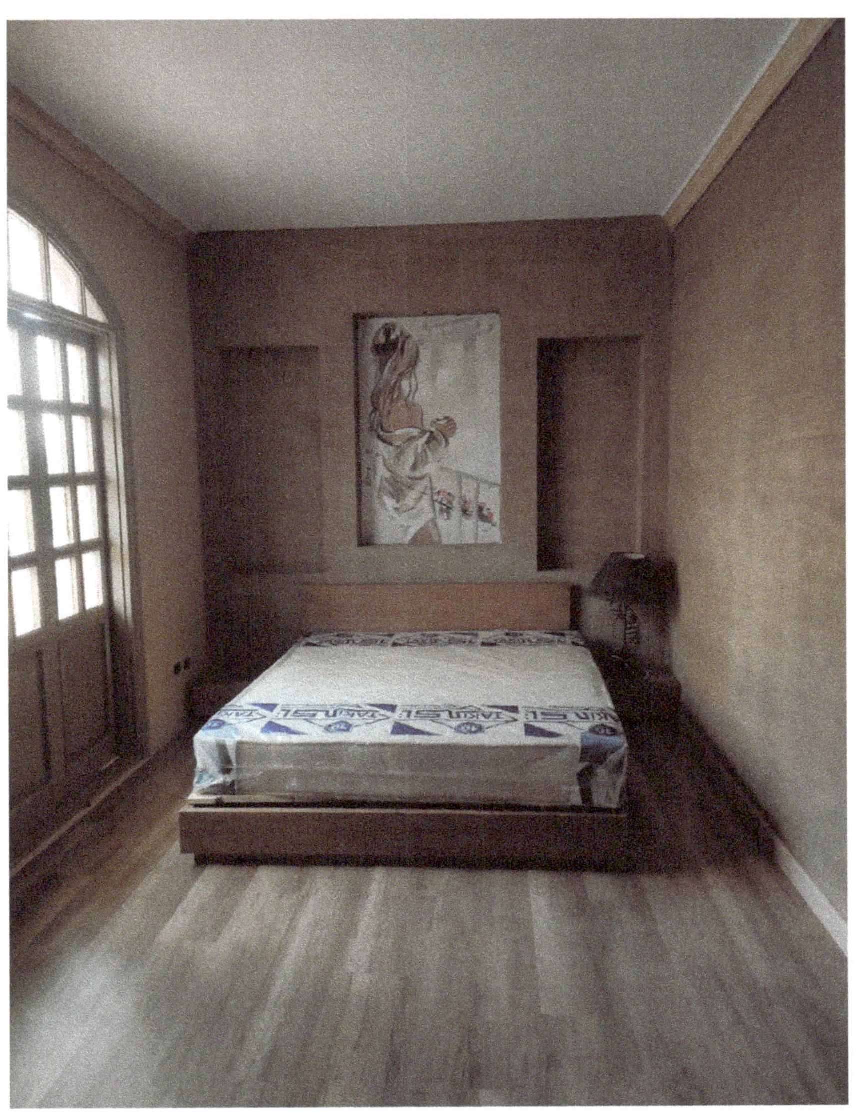

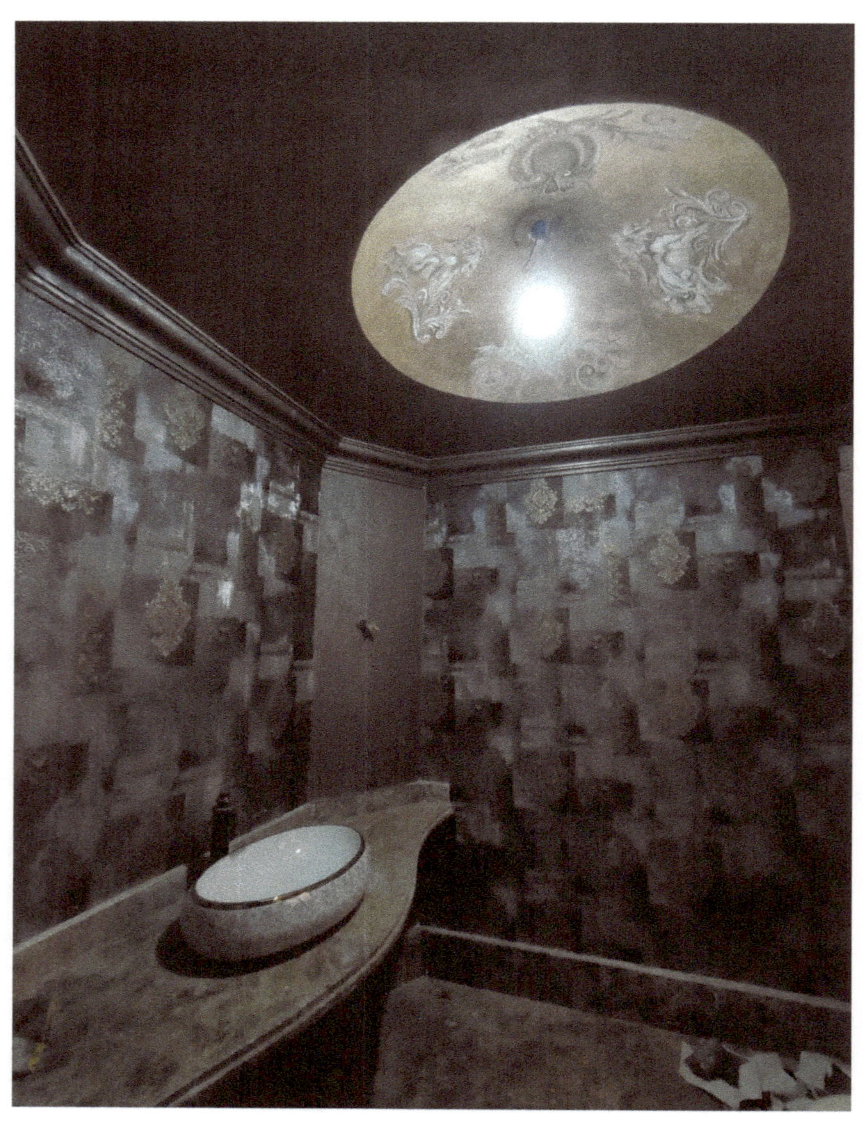

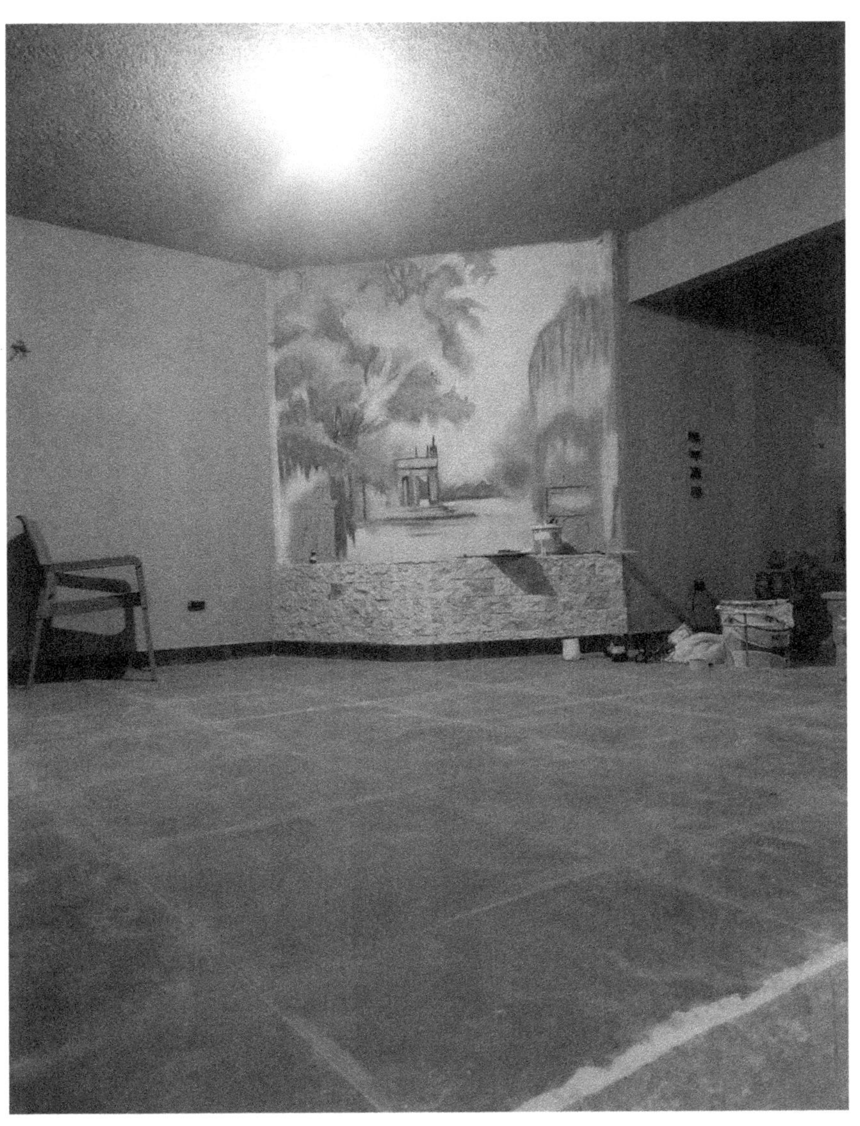

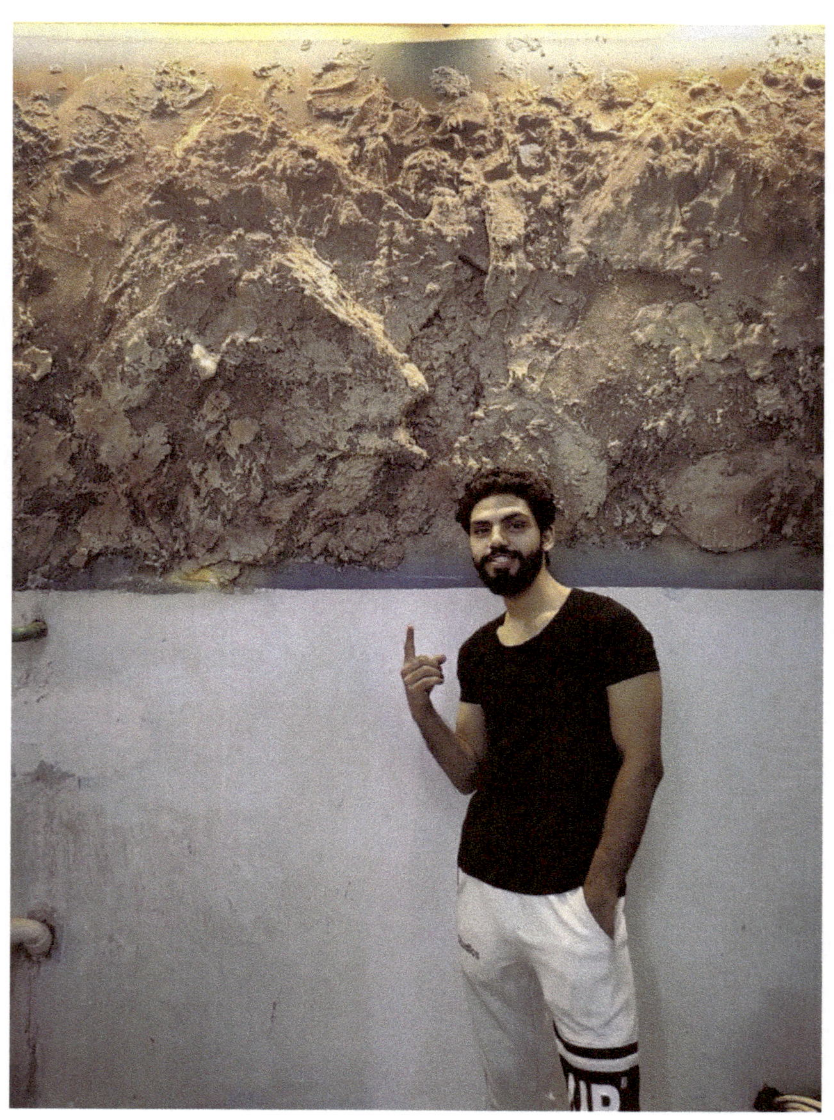

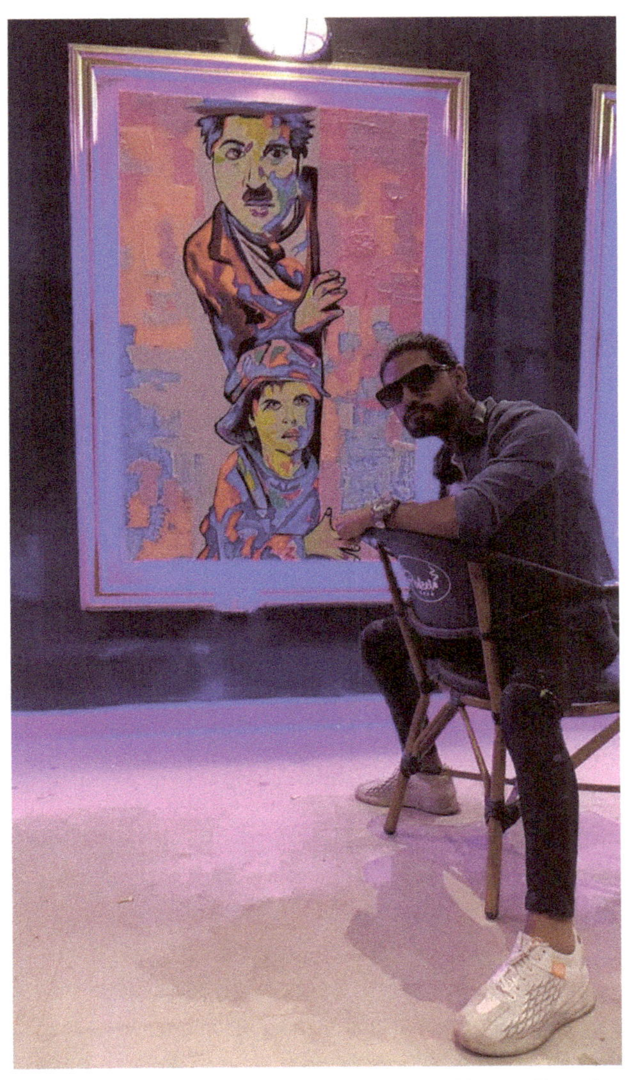

Egyptian culture, contemporary art, Karim Emad

CHAPTER 4

If art is any good, it has so much of a longer trajectory than
one night. Contemporary art is separate from art openings. In
the end, it depends on the strength of ideas in each piece.

—Elizaeth Peyton

Many artists believe that all art is contemporary, and Karim
Emad is no exception. The work of contemporary artists
explores several factors that give meaning and identity to their
artwork. Through their work, these artists express personal and
cultural identity, they offer critiques. The critiques presented are
most often about social and institutional structures. In general,
contemporary artists seek to also redefine themselves. In essence,
for artists like Karim Emad, everything is viewed as art, and they
believe that art is eternal. The timelessness of art causes all people
to reconsider conventional understandings in our society. In tun-
nels of creativity, audiences and admirers of the contemporary are
provoked to develop new forms of wisdom. Artist Karim Emad
is a contemporary artist at heart. Though he does not claim such
titles as he embraces his talent with great humility. His work leads
to unique creations that raise difficult questions without providing
easy answers.

For example, what does this painting mean? Who does this
painting represent? What is the message that is being conveyed by
artist Karim? In the past, I have frequently asked Karim these questions about his work, and his responses have only led me to my own

personal interpretations of his work. This chapter includes several examples of his contemporary pieces. They not only reveal Karim Emad's talent but also his imagination, an imagination that causes all those that meet him to reflect on their own worldviews and realities.

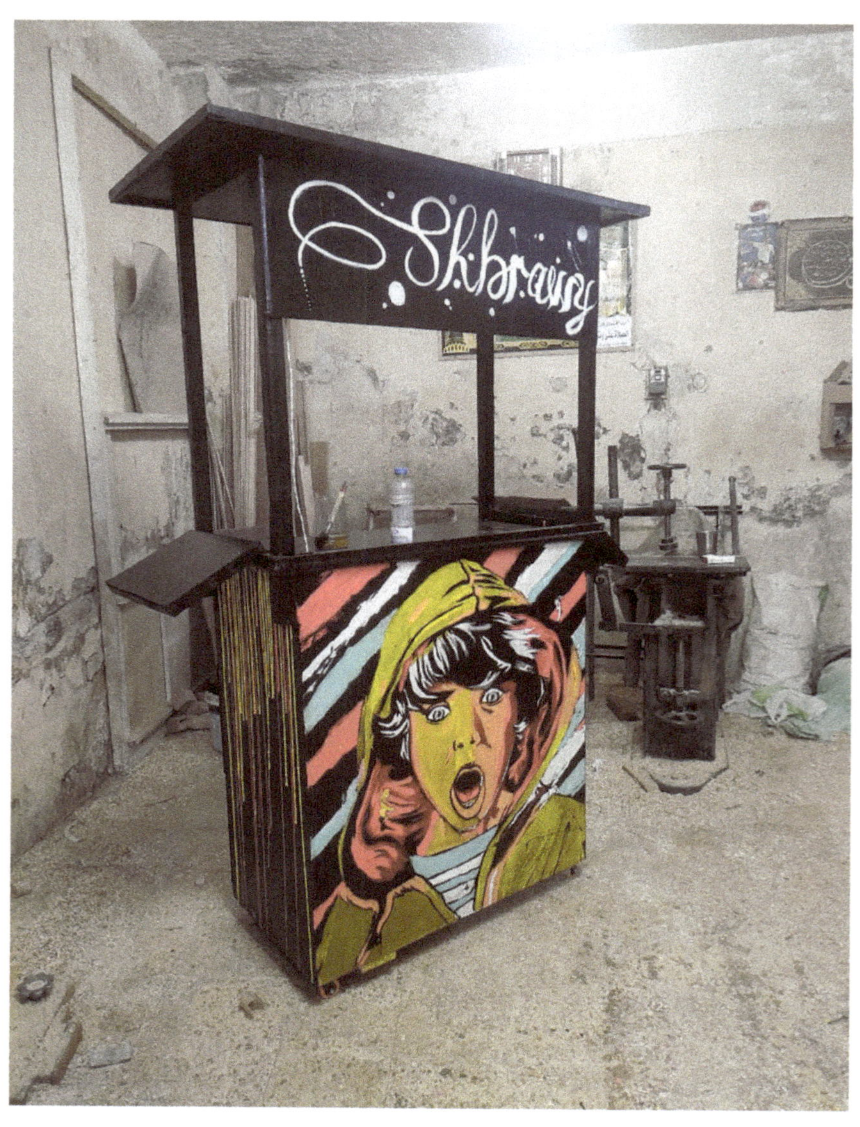

Sk.brawy

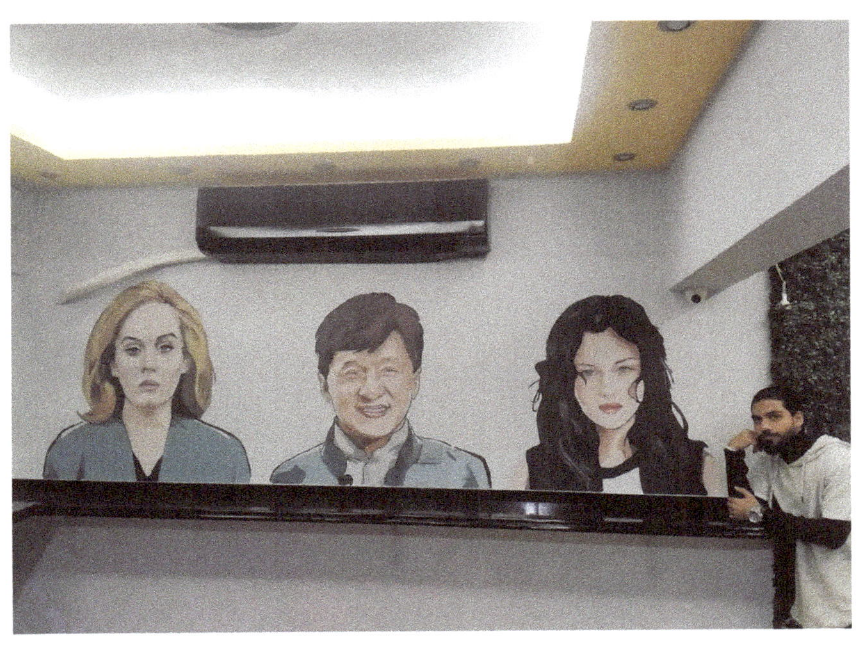

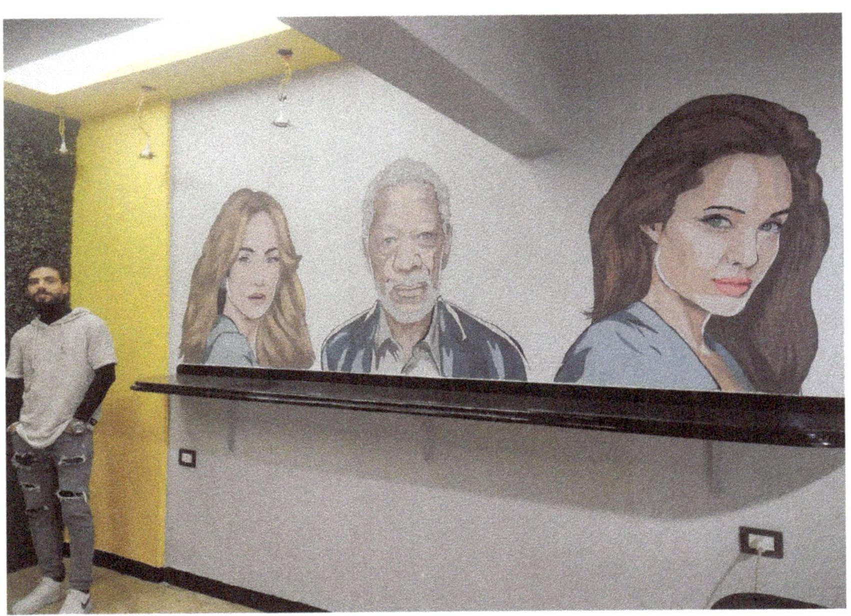

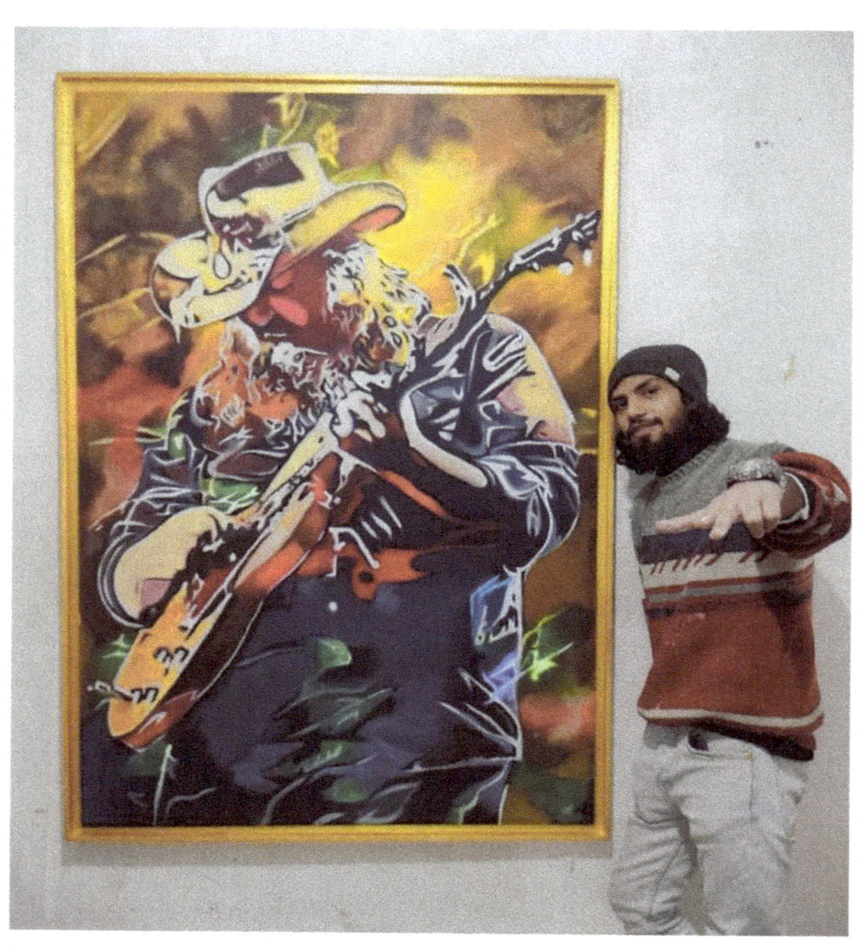

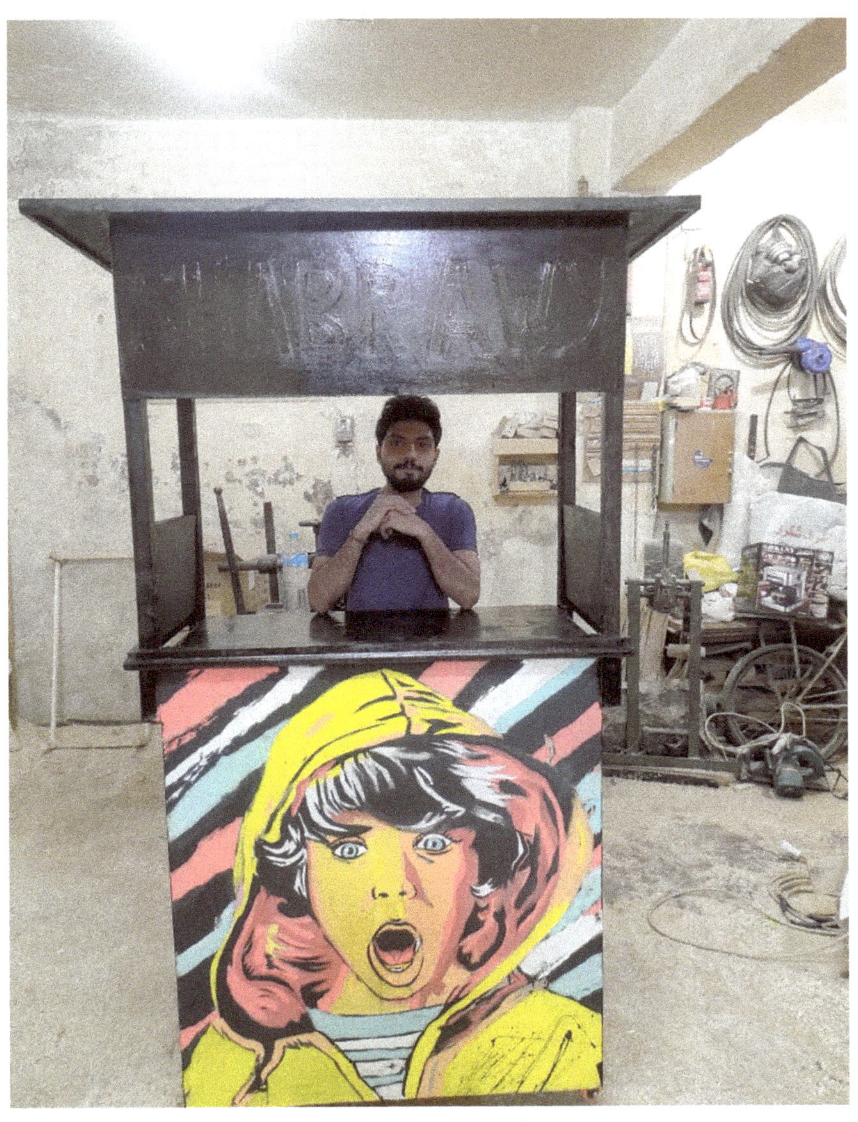

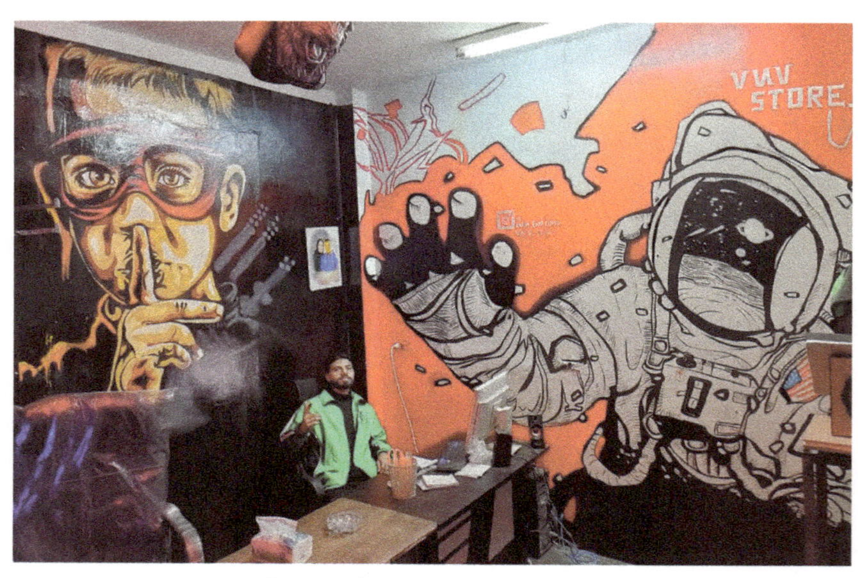

Postmodern art, Karim Emad

CHAPTER 5

A work can become modern only if it is first postmodern. Postmodernism thus understood is not modernism as its end but in the nascent state, and this state is constant.

—Jean-Francois Lyotard

The concept of postmodern art can be best described through symbolism. Its greatest feature is that it projects iconic symbols with unique gestures, giving it its own relevance and style, creating singular art pieces. Many artists have defined postmodern art by the use of new media and technology. They have identified three common themes in postmodern art: (1) parody; (2) humor; and (3) irony. Therefore, postmodern art rejects the traditional values of modernism and instead embraces conceptual art. The work of Karim Emad conveys this postmodern art style as he depicts his pieces through the means of social media and other flavors in art installations. His use of various social media platforms creates a unique and creative flare to his work through videos, music, and other types of performance art forms.

Karim has remained connected to American icons or styles in his work and given them their own existence in Egypt. He has filled walls, places, and canvases with their beauty and presence. In this chapter, we will see how Karim creates these masterpieces in his own light and perception. Clearly, he possesses the ability to maintain their authenticity as he paints them in his own postmodern style.

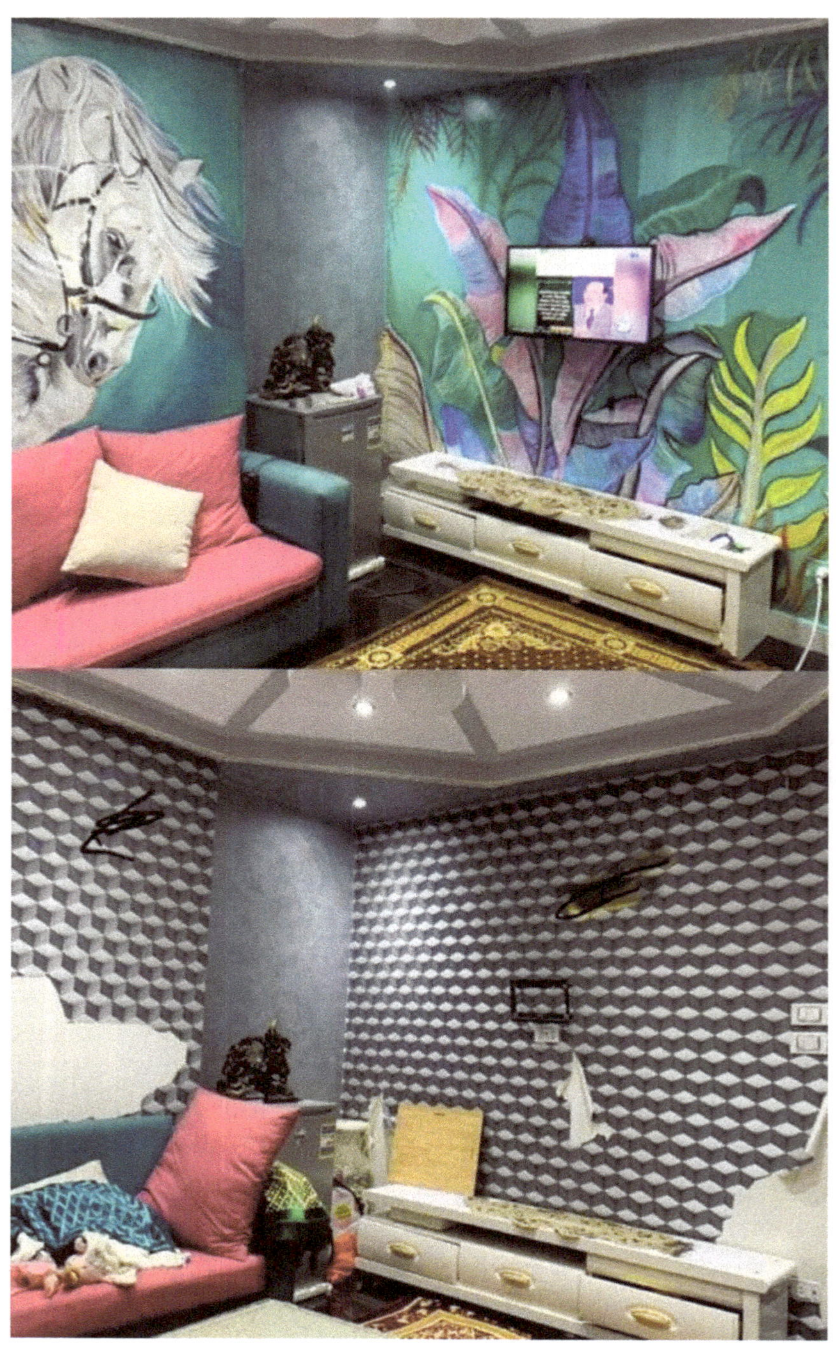

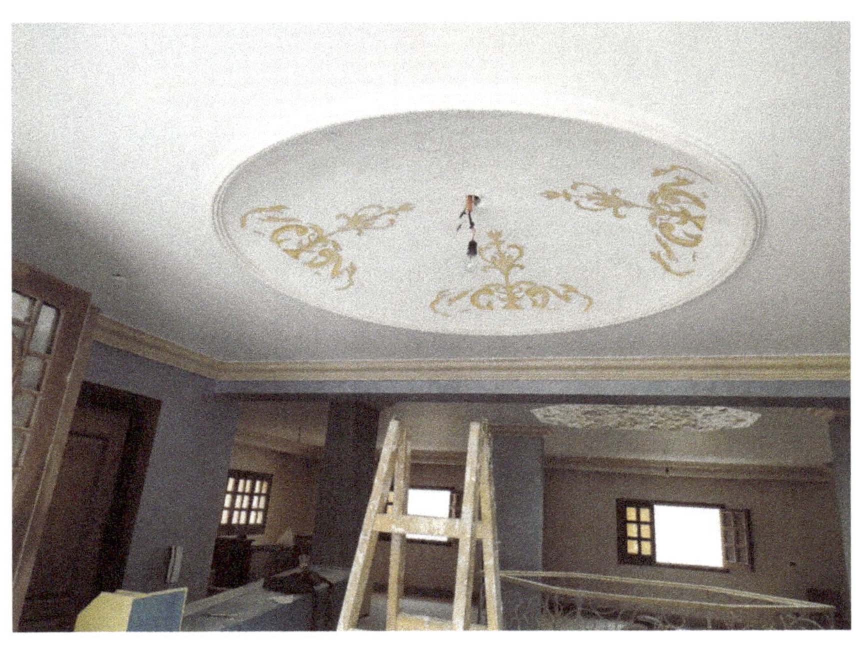

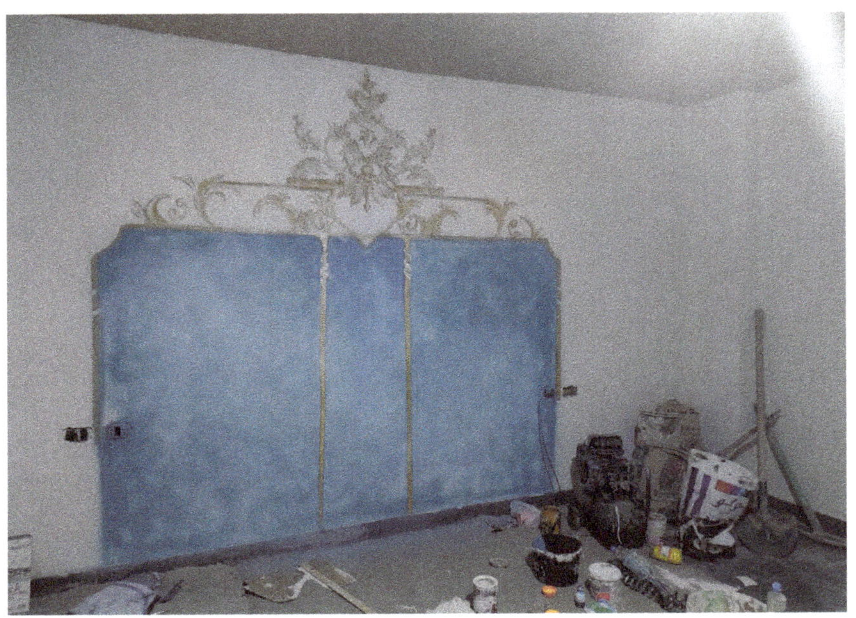

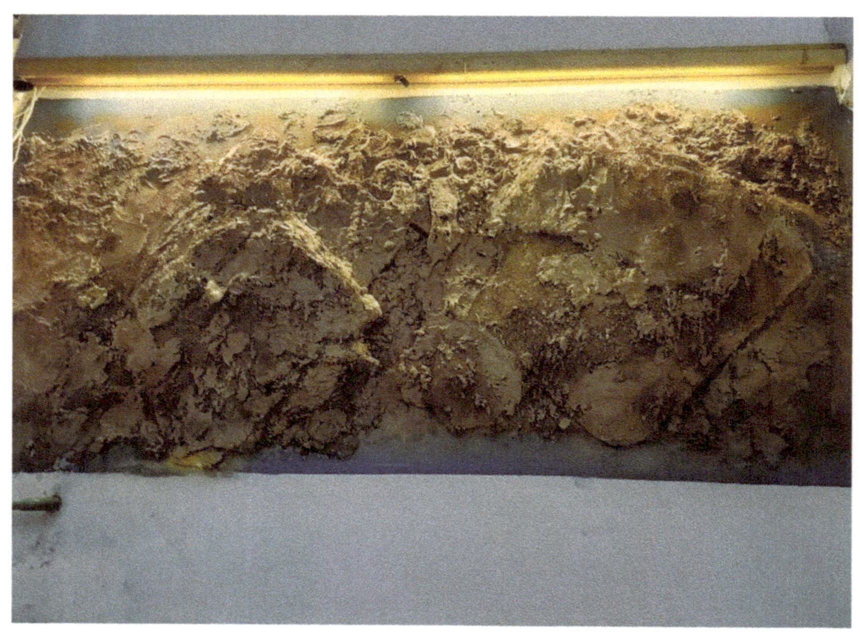

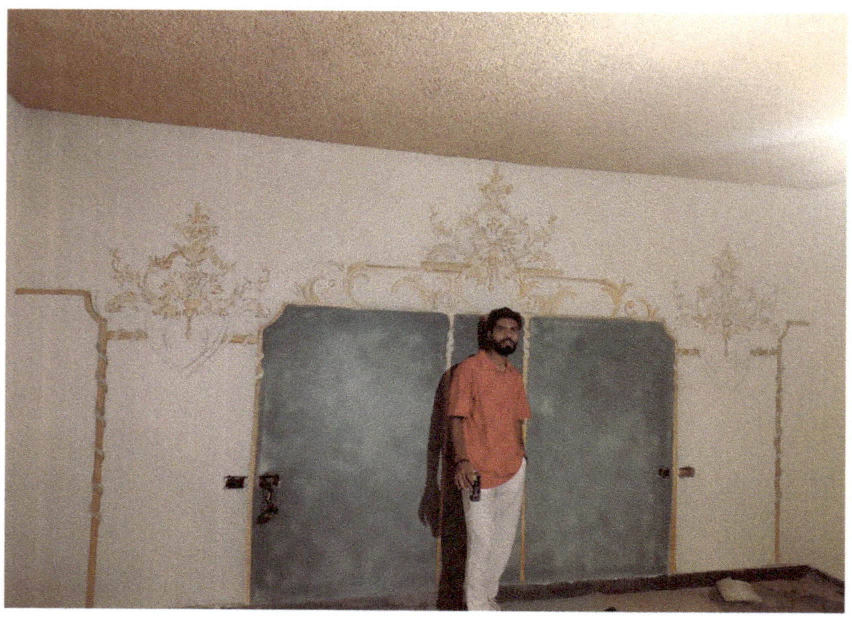

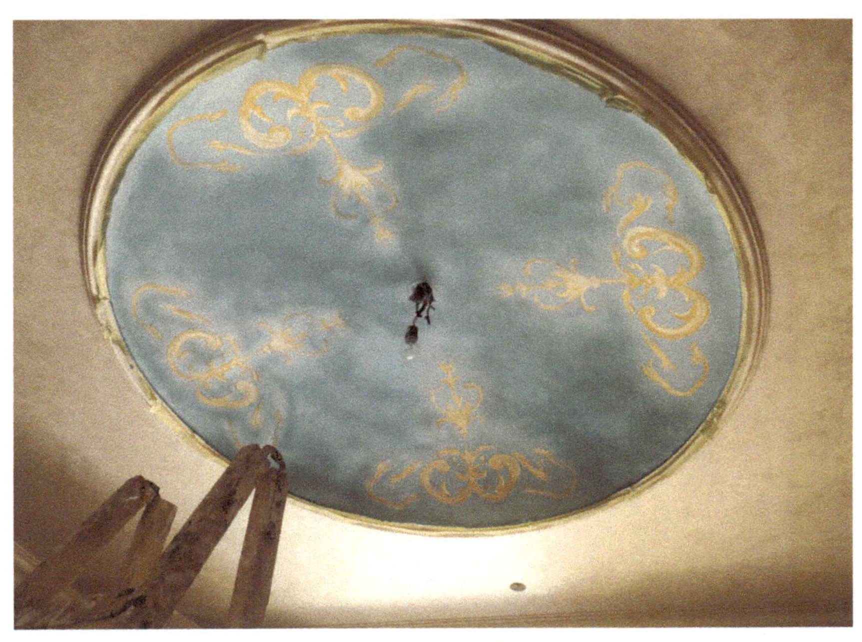

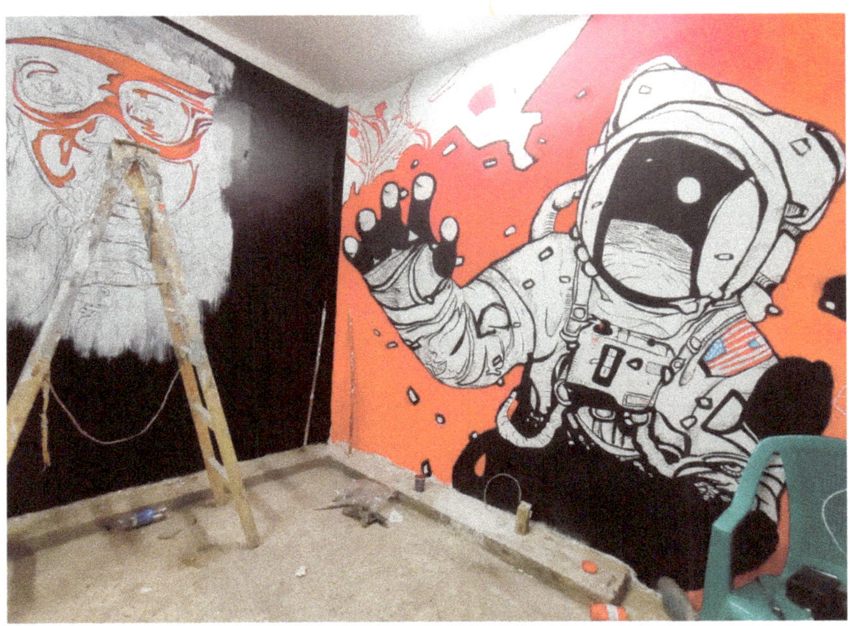

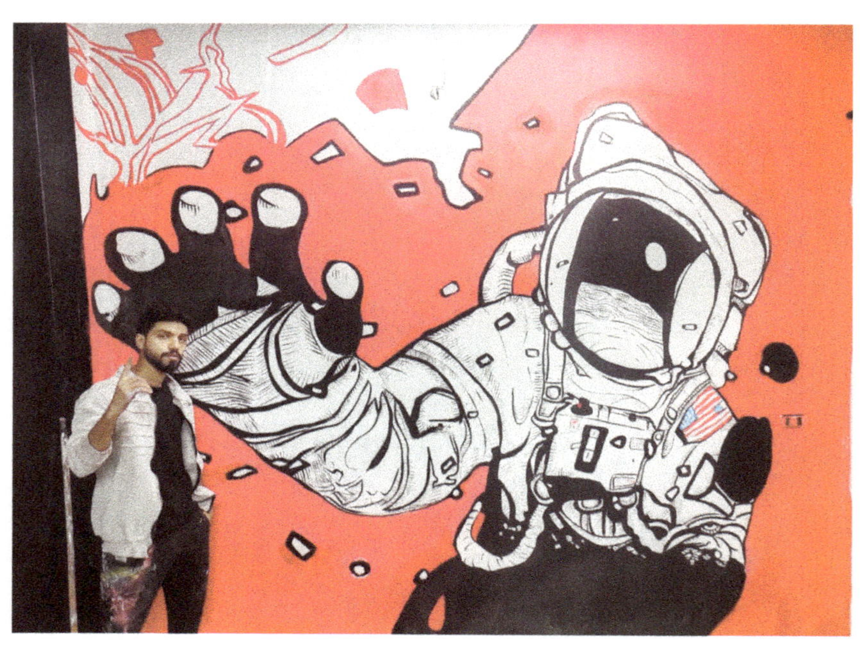

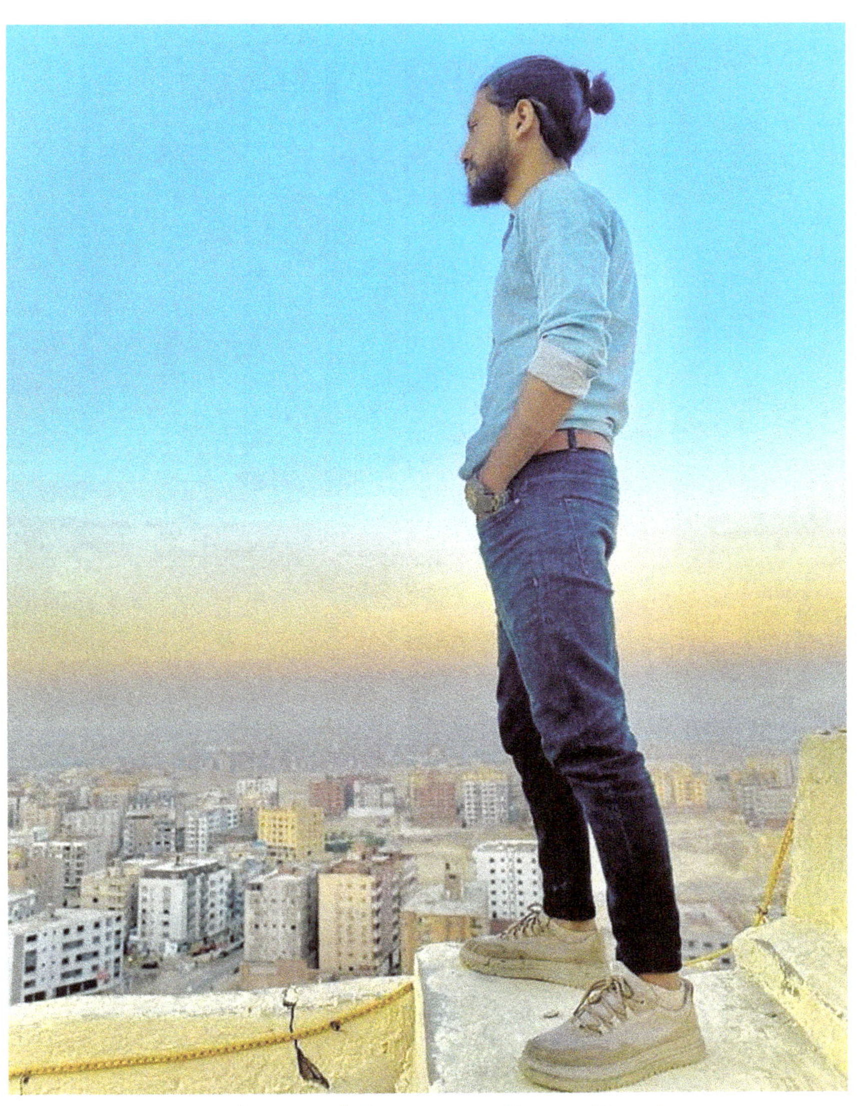

Reflections & Perceptions, Karim Emad

CHAPTER 6

The way we experience the world around us is a
direct reflection of the world within us.

—Gabrielle Berstein

Through the eyes of Karim Emad, I have experienced the world
of Egypt in the most beautiful and pure way beyond anything I
could have imagined. His art spoke to my heart and my imagination.
It helped me think beyond the enchanting videos of the pyramids
that I had watched in seminary. He introduced me to the postmodern Egypt, the one that longs for destruction, innovation, and reno-
vation, an Egypt that simply does not accept all truths and continues
to change the world with its timeless culture, places, and mysteries.
Truly, Karim Emad has given me the gift of a whole new world, a
world that is not limited by biases, fears, and differences. His art has
gifted me an expansion to my understanding of what it means to
experience human existence and suffering. As human beings, we all
seek to answer our deepest questions about life, God, and our world.
One could say that it may be what all of us have in common, regardless of language, culture, and religion.

As I reflected on all the ways in which Karim Emad has changed
my life, I realized that there are more mysteries in the spiritual world
that God wants us to discover. My relationship and knowledge of
God has only increased as a result of our union. I have discovered
that God gave us the gift of creativity and expression through art and
writing. These are gifts that are eternal in nature for all humanity

to enjoy and experience. In ending this book, I want to also share photography of Karim Emad that gives of a greater glimpse of his limitless talent and genuine spirit as part of my reflections on the eyes of Egypt!

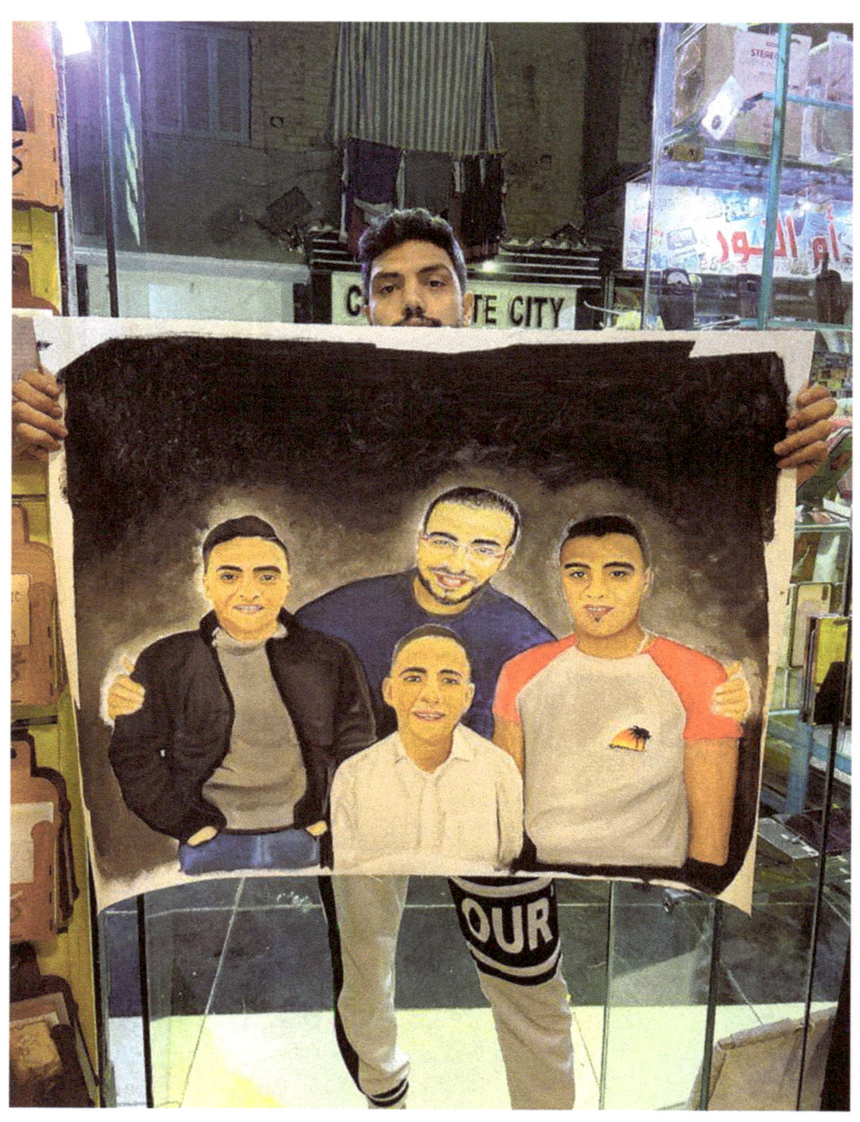
STEREO
CHOCOLATE CITY
أم الدور

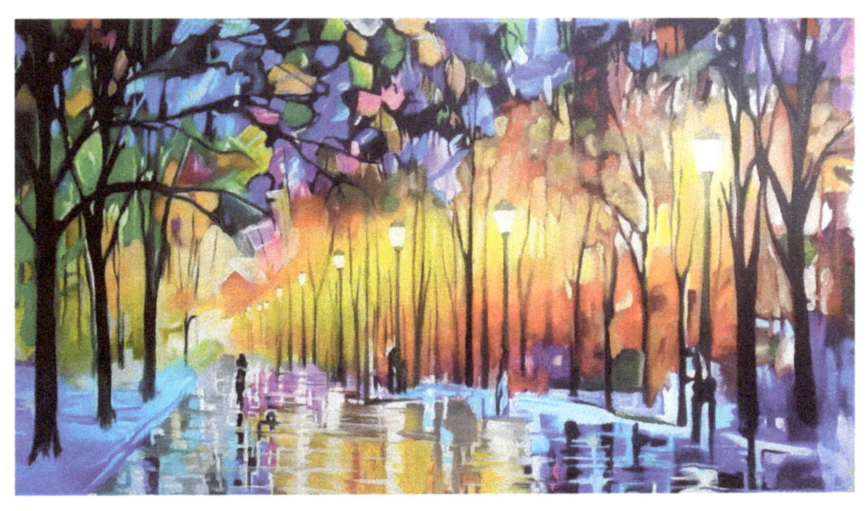

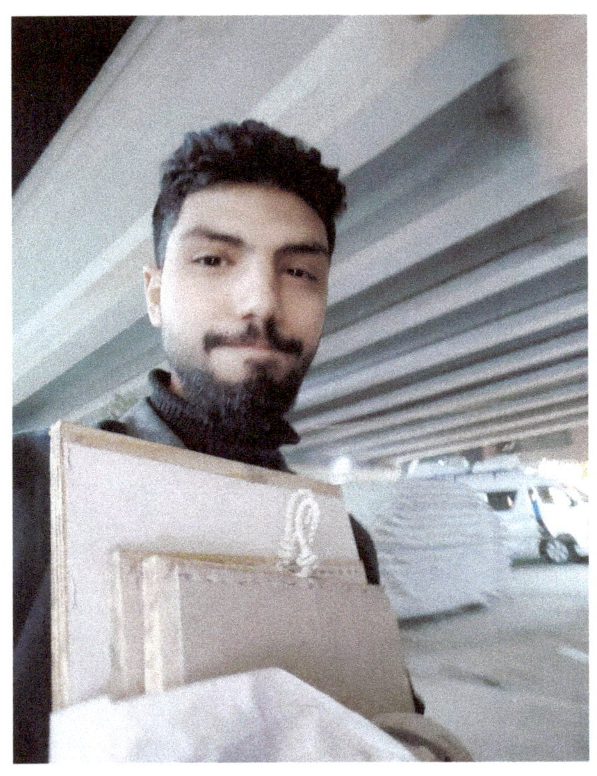

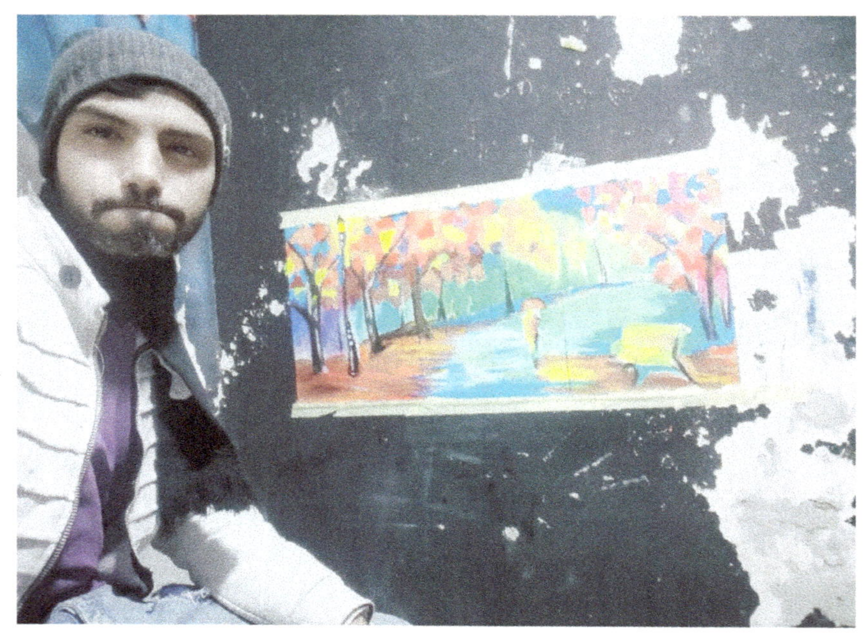

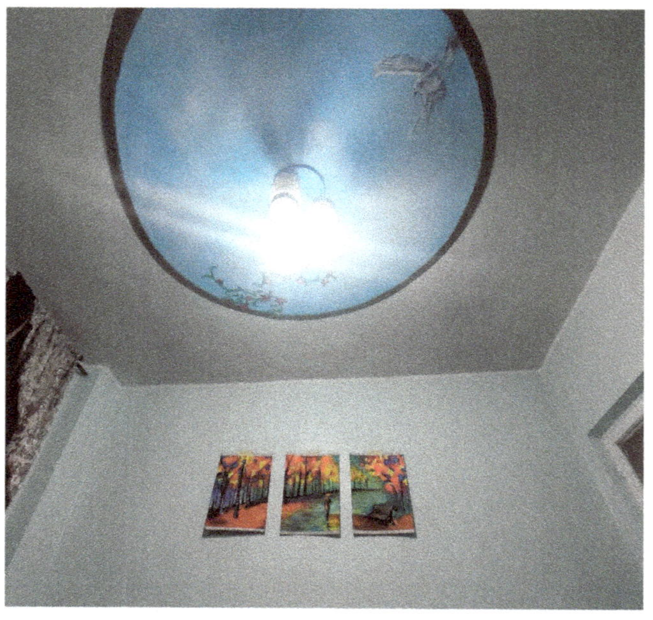

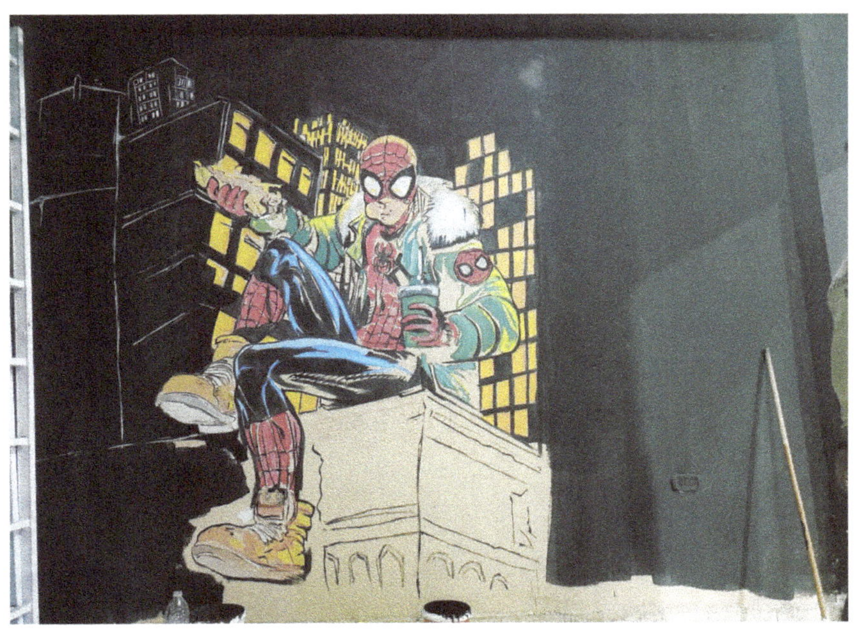

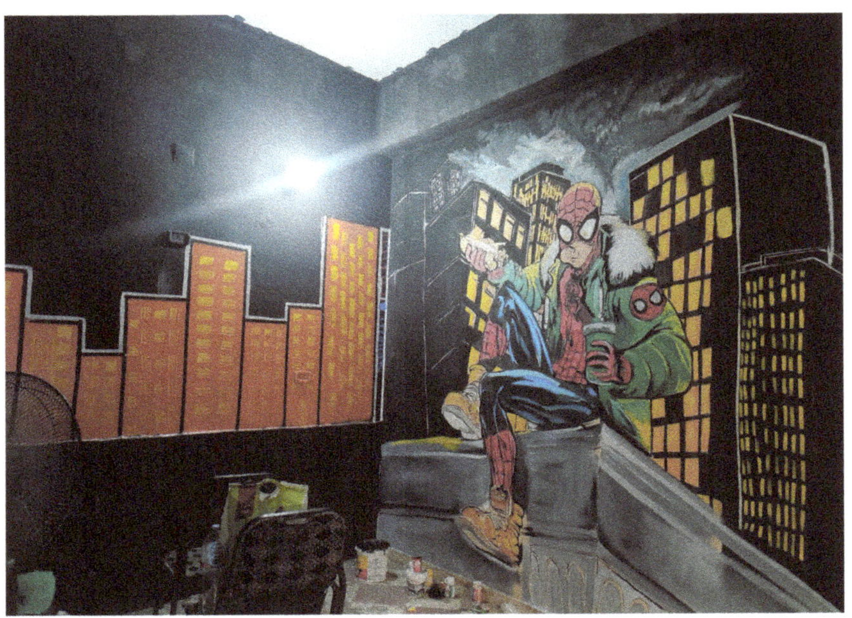

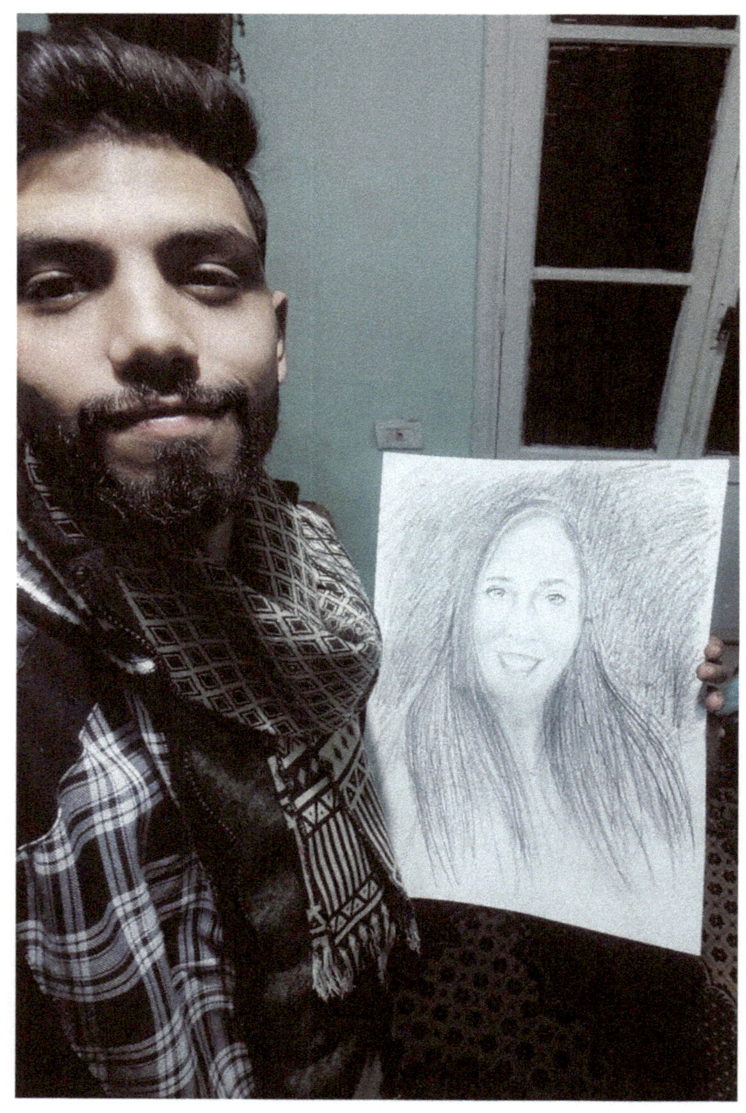

Conclusion, Karim Emad

CHAPTER 7

Reflection is one of the most underused
yet powerful tools for success.

—Richard Carlson

In conclusion, the power of art lies not just in its expression and versality. It is in its ability to stimulate our possibilities of reflection and imagination. In developing our knowledge of the various forms of art, we develop our potential for growing as individuals. We can grow in our understanding that we are truly intended to be co-creators with God in this enormous universe. I have come to learn from Karim Emad that God gives us all influence, but how we exercise it will make the ultimate difference. We are all given the ability to build others through our images, words, and innovations. How we use these tools will not only determine our success but also the global success of others.

For this reason, I decided to create this book with Karim Emad so that the whole world could have his published work of art, so that every person can be just as blessed as I have been through his paintings, drawings, and other forms of art. I wanted more than anything for people to know artist Karim Emad through his talent but also through his humanitarian spirit, a spirit that seeks to unite us all in spite of living in a world that insists on separating us all. Much like Karim, I long to live in a world where the love of God, the love of art, and the love of others will prevail across the land of Egypt and all nations around the world!

> *By living a life based on wisdom and truth, one can discover the divinity of the soul, its union to the universe, the supreme peace and contentment which comes from satisfying the inner drive for self-discovery.*

> —Egyptian proverb

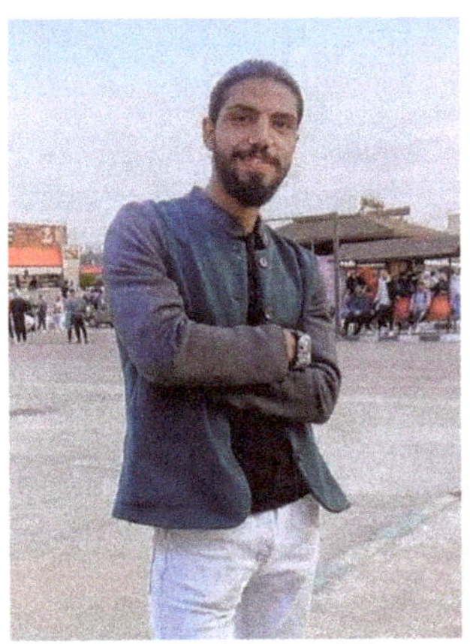

Karim Emad lives in Cairo, Egypt, with his devoted family. He is a professional and recognized artist that has developed his skills on various platforms. His passion is art but also enjoys sports and spending time in nature. He lives a life that seeks God and reaches others through the gift of art. He finds inspiration in everything.

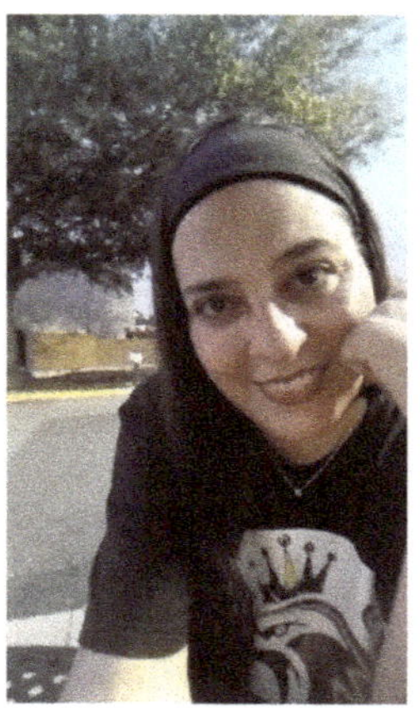

Lisa Camacho lives in Winter Park, Florida, with her devoted family. She is a medical social worker and minister to patients and families that are facing end-of-life issues. Her passion is seeking God, loving all of creation, and pursues providing inspiration to others.